Contents

Editor's Introduction

The Keswick Lectures were inaugurated in 1997 to provide in-depth analyses of issues of contemporary relevance, given by experts. Now published for the first time, this volume contains a great deal to make us think, pray and work. Editing the first Keswick Lecture book has proved to be both a challenge and a joy. The depth of insight and width of subjects covered in this book is awe-inspiring and provided me with a lot to think about as I sought to tighten up lanuage a little and ensure that sentences were sentences! These lectures were given over a five-year period and inevitably some of what we know now we didn't know then. But I have resisted any attempt to update them in the light of present knowledge. They have a great deal to say to us now, on subjects as diverse as mission, the church, the nations, the relevance of the Old Testament . . . Read and be changed by them.

Ali Hull
Bristol 2002

Chairman's Introduction

The Keswick Lectures have, in recent years, become a vital part of the Convention. As you look through the list of subjects I'm sure you'll agree they cover vital areas for the people of God to be considering. The lecturers are known for their expertise in their chosen areas.

I commend these lectures to you for your personal consideration, but also suggest to church leaders that they could form an excellent basis for a series of small group studies.

Peter Maiden
Chairman

The State of the Nation and
The State of the Church
by Clive Calver – 1997

CLIVE CALVER

In 1997, when Clive Calver gave two of the inaugural Keswick lectures, he was just embarking on a new career heading up the evangelical American relief agency, World Relief. Prior to that he had been the Director General of the Evangelical Alliance, which grew enormously in both size and influence under his leadership. Now based in Baltimore with his wife Ruth, he spends most of his time travelling from disaster area to disaster area, covering thousands of miles each year, and has been involved in Mozambique, Rwanda, Cambodia and Eastern Europe.

The State of the Nation

This is a two-part lecture. It doesn't naturally divide into the state of the nation and the state of the church, because I believe that the state of the church directly influences the state of the nation, and vice versa. Do you blame the darkness for being dark, or do you blame the light for not shining? The state of the church and the state of the nation will definitely overlap.

Marriage and divorce

I want to start by talking with you briefly on the subject of marriage and divorce. It was Marlon Brando who said, 'All but a few women wanted me to promise that their love would be returned in equal measure, and that it would be forever and undying. Sometimes I told them what they wanted to hear, but I have always thought that the concepts of monogamy, fidelity and everlasting love were contrary to man's fundamental nature.' Perhaps that's why England and Wales have the highest rates of divorce in Europe. Some 40 per cent of marriages end in divorce. In Britain today 25 per cent of all children experience their parents' divorce before they are sixteen years old. In the last two years, after the last major Divorce Reform Act came into force in 1996, the divorce rate doubled. The figures in 1993 were one hundred and sixty five thousand divorces in one year. Consequently, in 1993 the UK boasted, as I said, the highest divorce rate in Europe, almost twice the average. The proportion of unmarried women between eighteen and forty-nine who are co-habiting in Britain almost doubled between the start of the 1980s and 1994/5. The figure went up to 23 per cent, according to one statistic. The number of first marriages in the United Kingdom fell by nearly two-fifths between 1961 and 1993 to two hundred and ten thousand. In contrast, there were nearly seven times as many number of divorces in 1993 compared to 1961.

I realise that you love statistics, but I hope that they prove a point: we have a bad situation, and it's getting worse. 40 per cent of men and 34 per cent of women born before 1930 thought that co-habitation was wrong. If you were born between 1960 and 1978, the figure is not 40 per cent of men think co-habitation is wrong: the figure is 7 per cent. For women it's not 34 per cent think it's wrong, it's 6 per cent. And in 1993, fifty-five thousand children under five were affected by divorce in England and Wales.

We are living in a society where the old standards are dying. A private member's bill, due to become law next year, shortens the existing registry office vows to under four minutes long. Now Ruth and I will remember this, because we got married in a registry office twenty-five years ago today. My father-in-law was the Principal of London Bible College and we wanted to get married in the college chapel, and therefore we had to get married the day before in the registry office. And so we turned up in jeans to get married in the registry office and it was a fairly brief service to say the least, and then we waited until the next day and we got married the next day properly in the college chapel, and it did not last for four minutes. But the existing registry office vows are going to be reduced to under four minutes, the shortest ever wedding ceremony. I said, 'I solemnly declare that I know not of any lawful impediment why I may not be joined in matrimony to... I call upon these persons here present to witness that I do take thee to be my lawful wedded wife.' The new version will say 'I declare that I know of no legal reason why I may not be joined in marriage to... I take you to be my wedded wife.' This ridiculous change leads the *Guardian* to write, 'It's official. It now takes longer to heat a Marks and Sparks Chicken Tikka in the microwave than it does to get married.' Our society is shifting.

Sexual morality

Let's move on to a gentler and easier subject for us all: sex. I'll start off by quoting Charles Price, the Principal of Capernwray. 'It seems to me that there is a new morality emerging' Charles says, where good is basically honesty and integrity. If you are a homosexual, for example, be a homosexual. If you are going to commit adultery, do it openly. And bad is subtly described as hypocrisy and pretence, but is itself being redefined to include what has always been known in the past as self-denial and repentance. So to deny self in this new morality is to not be true to yourself, and therefore to be dishonest and hypocritical. So the church's task is not to catch the spirit of the age but to confront it, and to confront it with Christ, in whom lies not only the revelation of our inherent sin and inability to live as we should, but the possibility of forgiveness and the empowering of the indwelling life of Christ to live in such a way as to reveal the moral character of God.

That of course is not the general view. I wanted to get a nice gentle contrast to Charles Price, so I chose Boy George, who said, 'I don't see homosexuality as a curse or an affliction, though it is a cross of sorts. You are never going to convince anyone that you are happy defying God's so-called law, and anyway it's all down to personal interpretation.' What does that view lead us to? It leads us to a society that is somewhat different: where, on the Internet, you can now find the kind of pornography that would never see the light of day in your newsagent, with very little safeguard to stop anyone getting hold of it. Dr John Collie said in the *Observer Magazine* 'Accept teenage sex is a reality and learn to live with it.' And yet Dr Roger Ingham in the *Daily Mirror* disagreed and said, 'Most young girls I have interviewed said they regret how they lost their virginity and would love to turn the clock back.'

Spring Harvest had a clever idea, to interview three generations of my family. They took my mother-in-law, Connie Kirby, her daughter, Ruth my wife, and our daughter, Vicky. Vicky, who is just about to go to India to work with street kids and teach theology, has her mother's sense of honesty, so when you ask Vicky a question you get a straight answer. She was fourteen at the time. She was asked the question 'What is the most difficult thing you face at school?' She said, in front of her grandma, 'Explaining why I'm still a virgin.' You see, we are in a different kind of world.

There are still people outside of Christ who have a more healthy view. Paul Newman, the film actor, often would say of his very long-standing marriage, 'Why go out for a hamburger when you can get steak at home?' Probably not everyone gets steak at home, but you can get pretty bored with endless exotic take-aways. There are differing views on sex and morality, but our view nowadays is in such a minority as to be regarded by most as being totally old-fashioned.

Family values

What has this meant for the family? It has meant that the proportion of dependent children living in one-parent families in Britain has tripled since 1972. In 1994/5 1 per cent of children lived with just their dad, 19 per cent lived with just their mum. The average house-hold size in Britain fell to 2.4 in 1995 compared with 2.9 in 1971. This is partly because of increasing divorce rates and falling family sizes, as people, wondering what the future holds, have fewer children. Britain today has the highest rate of teenage pregnancies in Europe. Three out of every hundred fifteen to nineteen year olds have babies. The modern two parent family is increasingly a dual worker family. In 1993, 62 per cent of married women with dependent children worked or were seeking work, either full or part-time. Each successive group of new mothers is returning to the labour market more quickly than the one before. I do not say that to make a value judgement one way or the other, simply to comment that it is a changing facet within our society.

We have to recognise that today, as family values are adjusted, we also encounter the issue of who should be allowed to rear a family. The current debate over the adoption and fostering of children by gays, and how the church should respond to that issue, is perhaps highlighted by the interesting story of a lesbian couple and a gay couple who share a child they conceived between them by artificial insemination. The two-year-old boy spends the weekends with the two men and then Monday to Friday with the two women. One wonders quite what moral values that boy will inherit from his environment and his background.

Education issues continually trouble our country. Teachers can experience violence not only from pupils but also from their parents. As a result, leaders of the National Association of Head Teachers have called for new sanctions, which will allow for the expulsion of children whose parents have attacked a teacher.

Why?

It's an interesting environment in which we live. It's a changing family situation; it's a changing sexual situation; it's a changing situation in relation to marriage and divorce. I want us not just to concentrate on the whats; I want us to ask about the why. Why is our country in the situation it is in? As we look at issues of moral values together, I want us to ask why our country has adopted the value system that it has. We abdicate our responsibility and allow others to do our thinking for us. Sometimes we hide too glibly behind a text of Scripture, and we say 'This is wrong, because the Bible says it is wrong.' I agree with you, but the apostle Peter wrote, 'Let us learn to give a reason for the faith that is within us.' As evangelical Christians, we must start to think not just about how terrible our world is, but why it is so terrible, because if you go to that world and just say 'You are wrong' the first response will be 'Why?' I have seen so many letters written by well-meaning Christians to both the media and politicians in which Scripture is quoted verbatim, without any careful thought being given as to how those biblical references should be applied, and what they should be allowed to mean, and what in fact they would mean to the recipients of those letters. It is not enough to say, 'We have spread our bread upon the waters.' We have actually got to make our points constructive. We need to know why our society thinks as it thinks and feels as it feels, because there are reasons why. You are going to have to think with me, because this is going to be tough going.

The Enlightenment

It is my contention that the problem started in the eighteenth century, with what has come to be known as the Enlightenment. The

French philosopher, Voltaire, looked at the disastrous earthquake in Lisbon where ten thousand people died, and said, 'God, if there is a God, would never allow ten thousand innocent people to die.' Therefore Voltaire began to question that which had existed since the time of Christ: he began to question the basic presupposition of divine revelation. We think that what is wrong in our world is that our world isn't listening to what God has to say about it. Isn't that right? In other words, we believe what is wrong is that they're not listening to revelation, particularly revelation given in Scripture. The reason that they're not listening to that revelation started with Voltaire, because he and those like him began to say 'Revelation needs to be replaced by human reason.'

Let me take you to the eighteenth century Deist philosophers. They had a very simple idea. You see this lectern? Now the Deist philosophers would say, 'This lectern exists because it can be appropriated through your senses.' You can touch it; you can hear it; you can smell it; you can see it; and if you wish you can taste it. I'm not going to but you could. Now if I turned away, does this lectern still exist? If I can't use any of my senses to appropriate it, is it still there? Those views crystallised around a man named Bishop Barclay. And one of the wits of the day imagined a sycamore tree in the middle of a quadrangle in the university. He wrote this:

> There once was a man who said 'God
> Must find it most frightfully odd
> That this sycamore tree doth continue to be
> When there's no-one about in the quad.'

How can something exist if your senses don't appropriate it? Back came the response.

> 'Dear Sir, your astonishment's odd.
> I'm always about in the quad.
> And that's why this tree doth continue to be
> Since observed by yours faithfully, God'.

The Enlightenment placed the emphasis on human reason again. And it impacted every part of life. It impacted theology. That's where the whole of liberal theology, rational theology, comes from. That's where modernism originated. That's where the denial of revelation comes from, the emphasis on human reason. It's where Darwinism got its roots from. It's where the whole of what we call modernist thinking originated, and through the nineteenth century the church had to grapple with modernism. How do we grapple with human reason? How do we say that revelation is the way forward, revelation from God and not reason from man?

Modernism

Then cometh the twentieth century and human reason started to have some problems. Society was supposed to get better, because we were using our rational abilities, life was supposed to be improving, and it was in certain ways, we had science and technology, but there were kick-backs. It was a little hard to believe things were getting better after the battlefields of the Somme in the First World War. After the horrors of Hitler's gas chambers, it was hard to believe that human reason was the right way forward. The atom bomb was the death knell for what we call modernism or modernity in its classic form. It was the *reductio ad absurdum* of human reason. How could human reason be the answer when we could devise the way to destroy ourselves and our world several times over?

Then came my generation. I was four rows from the front when we stormed the American Embassy in Grosvenor Square to get peace in Vietnam: when we started to protest and shout, 'Make love not war.' We started to claim there had to be a different kind of way forward. Mine was the generation that overturned the ideas of human reason. We didn't go back to revelation; we moved on. We went to feelings. Samantha Fox ends up saying very simply, 'I give my body to the heat of the night, and who's to say if it's wrong or it's right.' That was before her encounter with Christianity.

Post-modernism

I once was trying desperately hard to explain to an Anglican vicar what happened to my generation, what led to what we now call 'Post-modernism'. I was really struggling. We were on the island of Jersey. Not exactly a hot-bed of filth and depravity, but as we walked across the market square there was an extremely attractive young lady, wearing a brightly coloured T-shirt. And as she got closer and I was engaged in earnest conversation with this vicar I noticed the slogan on her T-shirt, 'If it feels good, do it to me.' I said to the vicar, 'Now do you understand?' He said, 'I'm afraid so.' Welcome to post-modernism. You can see it in architecture; you can hear it in music; you can find it in literature; it's all around us. A post-modern world is not interested in if it's reasonable. It's interested in how it feels.

I want to introduce you to a very different kind of world. If you don't believe it exists, you need to have your TV set examined. It's the world of *Eastenders, Neighbours, Brookside*, tabloid newspapers, and increasingly the quality dailies as well. It is the post-modern world where each does that which is right in their own eyes. There is nothing new in this, it was around in the book of Judges, but now we call it post-modernity. I am my own *raison d'être*. I am my own justification of my own moral code. I do whatever turns me on. That is the thinking that under-girds life in Western Europe today.

I'm going to ask for a volunteer. Thank you sir, you look excellent. The gentleman with the beard, do you mind? You don't have to do anything, all you have to do is tell me your name – Jeff? – and tell me you don't mind me offending you. Forgive me for this, will you?

Our world looks at Jeff and thinks he's a perfectly normal kind of guy. And our world says of Jeff, if he wants to walk out of here and find a man on the way back to his accommodation and engage in a homosexual relationship with that guy, our world will say fine, if that's what turns you on, you go and do it. If Jeff wanted to leave here and find twenty-four women on the way back to his accommodation and engage in all kind of activities with them, our world would marvel at his athleticism and it would wonder at his stamina, so probably would Jeff, but they wouldn't condemn him. If Jeff wants to have a wife and two point four children in an average nuclear family, the only thing our world will wonder about is where he got the point four from. Our world is quite happy for Jeff to live as Jeff wants. Neither way is right or wrong. It's just Jeff's right or Jeff's wrong. Jeff is told to be true to Jeff. Our world doesn't mind if Jeff finds God through Buddha, Marx, Mohammed or Jesus, because no way is right, it's just what is right for Jeff. That's what our world believes. Can you see how dangerous this is for us? We've got people going around today saying, 'We are going to be persecuted any minute.' I don't believe a post-modern world will persecute us for being Christians. Our world's quite happy if Jeff's a Christian. It says 'Jeff, we do hope you have a wonderful meeting, we hope you enjoy your Convention; we hope you have a super time.' Our world's perfectly happy about it. The only thing our world will worry about is if Jeff tries to put Jeff's truths on them.

No absolutes

If you would really like to be persecuted I'll tell you how you can do it. All you've got to do is say to our world not 'I've got a better way' or 'Have you found Jesus?' or 'The Bible speaks about an alternative way of living' – but 'You are wrong.' And you'll be persecuted. You're allowed to do and believe anything you like today, providing you don't try and share it with anybody else. That's the awesome danger of our post-modern world. It has denied the existence of any absolutes. Everything is relative. Each does what is right for them. The breakdown of the family; the breakdown of God's standards on sexual morality; the breakdown of marriage, all lie at the door of that one simple concept: 'I do what is right for me.'

Scripture says something different. I was preaching this in Bradford Cathedral at the start of this year, and during the interval a lady came up with her fifteen year old daughter, an extremely attractive young girl. She asked, 'Can you help my daughter? I can't answer her question, can you?' I said, 'I'll try.' The daughter said, 'How dare you tell me what I should do? How dare you say that if my friends want to be gay they're wrong? How dare you say that there's a right and wrong way to live for everybody? How dare you put your truth on me?' Now she was a very nice girl. She wasn't being nasty; she was just speaking for her generation.

She said, 'Each of us have got to do what's right for us.'

I said, 'Fine, you've been listening to your generation, haven't you?'

'Yes.'

'This is what all your friends believe, isn't it?'

'Yes.'

'Okay, so everything is right, each person can do what they like?'

'Yes.'

'All right, so I go out of Bradford Cathedral here tonight, I find a five-year-old boy, and I engage in an act of buggery with that five-year-old boy, am I right or wrong?'

'You're wrong!'

'Look, once upon a time there was a line, and there was a marker in the middle of it, and everything on the right of that line was wrong and everything on the left of the line was right.'

'Yes, I know, people used to believe that.'

'And you don't believe there's a line any more?'

'No.'

'But you just said I was wrong. It's not that the line doesn't exist any more, the line's still there. All you've done is you've moved the marker. Your generation has moved the marker as far to the right as you can, so that everything is right for you that you want to do, and it's only the poor little paedophile that gets left out in the cold, because you'll allow everything else.'

The nonsense of relativism is that there is still a line. There is still right and wrong, but it has now become a matter of convenience. I believe that somehow we have got to get back to the only line that genuinely has always existed and still exists, and that is the line contained in this book. Because I don't believe this is a book for Christians. That's one of the lies of our society. They say, well, Hindus have the Bhagavad-Gita, Muslims have the Koran, you Christians have your Bible. I don't believe that. Do you believe in the God Who created heaven and earth? Do you believe that He is the Lord of all of humankind? Do you believe that He has revealed His will for how we should live in His world, His way, in the pages of Scripture? Then this isn't a book for Christians, it's a book for everybody. If you want to live in God's world, God's way, you've got to get back to Scripture. We've got to get away from relativism. We've got to get back to the absolutes that God has laid down. We've got to get back to biblical truth as it is revealed and we've got to proclaim it in a way that our world understands and understands why we need to live in that world that way.

Grace and truth

That's a very strong message, and if you're going to do that, you're going to have to earn the right to do it. Let me tell you how you earn the right to do it. You earn the right to do it in the way that Jesus did. Jesus took truth and lived it, and He combined it with grace. A friend of mine once said, 'I read in Scripture about a man named Jesus who went about full of grace and truth. Why is it that some of His people have got more truth than grace, and others have got more grace than truth?'

If you believe that this world's in a dreadful state, if you believe that the state of our nation is just going miles away from what God intended, then the answer is very simple. You've got to hold to truth in one hand and live with grace in the other. There is no other answer to this world. And if we're going to live with grace it's going to mean something to us. To some of us it will mean opening our homes to the prostitute on the street corner to show grace alongside truth. It does not mean that you deny the truth of what you believe, it means that you have the grace to confront people living in a way you do not believe they should live, with the truth that comes when they can see the grace. I always found that the gay programmes would come and talk to me, because they knew I would always say they were wrong, but I would always do it with sympathy and concern and be prepared to listen to them. I would never give an inch in conceding ground to them, but I would always try to be warm, open, ready to listen and offer a cup of coffee.

Somehow in this world we've got to do something to make a difference. I'm not saying this to give any credit to my family. Some years ago a girl arrived on our doorstep. She came for a day and she left years later. She was dressed like a boy. She'd got her hair short like a boy. She was flat-chested; she looked just like a boy. After the first time she sat in a room alone with me at night she said to my wife the next day 'I don't understand why Clive didn't abuse me, he's the only man except my father who never has tried to do that.' She had been abused as a child more often than she could remember. She had become a Christian many times. The problem was the only way she knew how to give love was with her body, and so it just kept going wrong. I could have preached to her. I've got some really good sermons for people in that condition. I could have given her one of the very best. My wife did not think that was what was needed. Ruth thought what was needed was actually that this girl should have a home. My daughter Vicky at the time was nine years old. She was just going into her own room for the first time. You know what that's like, when your child — and we've got four kids — is just going into her own room for the first time. Vicky said of this girl 'I think she should live with us, she can have my room, I'll stay with my baby sister.' That girl lived with us for the next three years until I threw her out. I threw her out because she'd got a professional qualification and she went off and got a job, lived in a flat, was part of the local church, and then she met this guy, fell in love and I had to do the wedding. I nearly didn't make it through that wedding. I just about got there. I had the privilege two weeks ago of dedicating their second child. Now they're planning to go off and work overseas full time for the Lord Jesus. That is not because we mouth truth. It's because we've got to live grace.

There are so many issues that we've got to take on board, but we've got to live them and not just speak them. We've got to demonstrate that compassion and commitment. Let me take a simple issue for you. My closest friend is a guy named Lyndon Bowring, he's the Chairman of CARE Trust, and Lyndon always shudders when he hears me say something like this, because I will start off by saying 'I don't believe that any evangelical Christian has got the right to be against abortion', and I'm as pro-life as the next person so you need to wait for the next bit, because the next bit is 'Unless they're prepared to open their home to the single parent; to co-operate with an adoption agency; to extend their own family; or to encourage the work of those who can do that, like CARE and others, and to pray that the church might do and not just speak.'

That's where grace and truth come together. Our world is desperate for a message of truth, but it will only accept it when it sees love in our lives, love in our eyes and in our hearts: a people burning for God, passionate for Him, determined to serve Him, being ready to live in grace. You may say, 'I'm not in a position to do that.' But you can pray. Some of you have been praying for years, haven't you? You've not just looked and condemned, you've poured out your heart to God in prayer. Others of you have done so much quietly in the background and I wouldn't know anything about it, but that's the kind of church we've got to be if we're going to change things. Our world is desperate. It's desperate for truth and it's desperate for life.

Are all faiths the same?

Let's just look at other faiths. We're now living in a society where we have half a million people who belong to other faiths. We're living in a society where we are told those half million have a perfect right to stand on an equal footing with us, and I want to say 'What do you mean by an equal footing? Are you saying that each faith is as right as the next one?' I had to take a meeting in Cambridge University in Trinity Great Hall. It was packed with students. The subject was 'Buddhism, Islam, Christianity, it's all the same thing, isn't it?' It was a Sunday night and the room was packed. Muslims, Buddhists, Sikhs, Hindus and the odd Christian who'd skipped church. I stood there and said 'Look, you've got to judge a faith by what it claims. Other faiths claim to tell you about God, but Christianity claims to introduce you to Him. Therefore if Christianity is real and true, it goes further than any other faith because you can meet God, not just know about Him. Therefore you need to examine the claims of Christianity first. All faiths are different.'

Let me try to demonstrate that to you for just a moment. Now this is one of those awful points where I ought to have my texts and I haven't, so here goes. Islam, Judaism and Christianity say there is one God. Hinduism says there's many gods, Buddhists search for reality in themselves. Is it one faith, are they all the same? Jewish thought has no concept of original sin. Buddhism denies the possibility of sinning against a supreme being. Muslims have an idea of sin, so they have a strong moral code. Hinduism has no concept of sin. Christianity recognises the existence of Satan, the presence of sin, but also the possibility of forgiveness. It was Peter Cotterell, when he was at London Bible College, who said, 'Truth is not a matter of pride or humility, it's a matter of fact. Islam says that Jesus wasn't crucified; we say He was. Only one of us can be right. Judaism says that Jesus wasn't the Messiah; we say He was. Only one of us can be right. Hinduism says that God's often been incarnate; we say only once. We can't both be right.' Any intelligent person could decide that all religions are wrong. Any intelligent person could decide that one is right and the rest are wrong. But no intelligent person can seriously believe that all religions are essentially the same. They aren't. And Krishna said, 'The problem I have with Christianity is that Christians show no more signs of being saved than anyone else does.'

Dialogue

If we live the message, we can speak the truth. We can meet those of other faiths; enjoy their food, as I do because I love curries; be prepared to dialogue with them, to work with them; but don't compromise on truth. We don't want a dialogue with other faiths that says we're all the same. We want a statement to other faiths that says we respect you as people, but we beg to disagree. We are in a society that says, because of its post-modernism, disagreement is wrong. I shouldn't say this and I'll get in trouble for it, but up until recently my wife was a member of the Labour party. I know she's wrong, but I still live with her. Somehow we've got to learn how to disagree with dignity. Somehow we've got to learn how to disagree without being disagreeable. Somehow we've got to learn to confront our world where it's wrong, but to go there with the love of Jesus. Somehow we've got to learn how to get our hands dirty by meeting people who are poor, dispossessed, living immoral lives, but love them with the love of Jesus and don't compromise the truth to them. That's the only way we're going to arrest what is happening in our country. What happened in the church was we withdrew into our evangelical ghettos. We 'came ye out from among them and [we] became separate' because then we would be untainted. Post-modernism needs a dialogue that says, 'You are wrong and this is why you're wrong.' You try facing Ludovic Kennedy with that kind of stance. But you can do it, because God will give wisdom and grace. You can do it in your local community. You can pray for local needs. You can meet people and show them the love of Christ. You can get involved with their needs and their hurts in so many ways, as you demonstrate that you've found somebody who's changed your life.

The state of our nation is only going to get worse for as long as it maintains that human reason is the answer. Now it's gone further and said human feelings are the answer. We've got to get back to the fact that there is only one answer and His name is Jesus. He alone is the truth, and the way, and the life.

This is our world, in a desperate plight: family life falling apart; marriages empty in so many cases; kids suffering all the time. People of other faiths are being abused and put down instead of being dialogued with, or they're being endorsed when they need correction. We are failing to meet the issues of our day. People are lapsing into addiction and self-indulgence. Who is the answer? Jesus. Who gives the answer? The church. What is our duty? Just to go and change our world. Just chuck your salt on the water. You may never see what happens. God gives the underground earthquake because He is God. And as Corrie Ten Boom, that lovely Dutch saint said once, 'When I enter that beautiful city, and the saints all around me appear, I hope that somebody will tell me it was you who invited me here.' Please brothers and sisters, this is a post-modern world that needs to get back to divine revelation and away from human feelings. Please would you go and change your world.

The State of the Church

'The State of the Church' is the single most contentious issue I am talking about here this year. I am reasonably comfortable that I probably know more than most of you about the state of the nation, and you believe that. When I talk about the state of the church you will probably not believe that I know more than you do, because your understanding of church is your bit of it. Most of you belong to one of the twelve tribes of evangelicalism in Britain today, and believe that your tribe is the true Israel and that others have something to learn from you. They probably do, but that doesn't mean that you hold a monopoly on truth.

The divisions of the church

If you are looking at the state of the church in Britain today, you are not looking at a homogeneous whole. You are looking at a number of divisions, covered by that word church. The church in Britain, firstly, has a whole liberal section: those who would not accept the literal truth of Scripture, who would not regard the Bible as being the ultimate rule for our faith and conduct. You are only looking at just over ten per cent of churchmanship in this country, but it is still an enormously influential ten per cent and it still affects much.

Remember when we were talking about the state of the nation, I spoke on the irrelevance, or just plain wrongness, of the supernatural when looked at from a liberal perspective; the understanding of Jesus as other than Son of God, and above all the concept that all faiths have equal value in a post-modern world. I remember desperately trying to debate with the multi-faith group that put together a paper on proselytising, because they began from the perspective that said it is wrong to impose your opinions on someone else. I have a lot of sympathy with that, I have to confess. I don't believe we have the right to impose our opinions on others, whether we are right or wrong. This group had put together a forty page paper, urging ways in which proper controls should be exercised in seeking to reach those of other faiths with a different faith. In other words, all of that was cautionary on proselytising, or what we would call evangelism. Much of it we could learn from in terms of not forcing our beliefs on others. The cudgel I took up was that there were forty pages warning against imposing our opinions on others, but nothing at all, not one single mention, in terms of protection for people who chose to convert to another faith. Somehow that's the *reductio ad absurdum* of the whole liberal method. We want to allow all things providing they're not absolute. The only absolute is that there aren't any absolutes. Everything must be tolerated except something that demands that it is an absolute truth. That is intolerance in itself, that the liberal has within their own creed the seeds of their own destruction, because they'll allow everything except where you and I are coming from, and that's tragic.

The second group within the church is the Catholic. It comes in two sections; Roman Catholic, originating way back to the church of the first five centuries, and its other stream is the Anglo-Catholic, with its emphasis on ritual and an expression that relies totally on liturgy and on tradition, a hearkening back to the days of the apostolic fathers. The third tradition, the Orthodox tradition, is not very large in our country, but very, very large worldwide.

The fourth tradition, broad churchmanship, is another of the ones that I have some problems with. The idea here is that all perspectives can be accommodated because it is actually a good thing to go to church, and it is actually respectable to be churchgoing and believe the right kind of things, providing you don't get enthusiastic about it. But if I'm not enthusiastic about a Christ who died for me, a Lord who has come to live in my life by His Holy Spirit, about Scripture and all that it gives me to live in God's world, God's way, then my faith is pretty poor. I confess to being an enthusiast. They accused evangelicals of enthusiasm throughout the nineteenth century, and I'd love them to start doing it again today. If you ever ask me when things started to change in churchmanship in Britain today, I would say it was when we recovered the capacity to smile in church; when we actually realised that we could be normal before God, that He loves us as we are, and you are quite entitled to be enthusiastic about Jesus.

Evangelicals

Those are the four strains. You may say 'You have missed the fifth one.' Yes, I have, and that's the evangelical. The evangelical strain, very simply, believes that the Bible is the word of God, that Jesus is the Son of God. It holds to the traditional creeds of the church and owns a personal commitment to Jesus Christ in the life of the individual where He comes to reign as Lord and King. Dr David Bebbington, in his brilliant book *Evangelicalism in Modern Britain*[1] says that traditionally evangelicals are four things:

- They are conversionists. They believe that someone has got to come to a belief in Christ. It may be a process, it may be a crisis, but either way, an evangelical believes they have been converted.
- They are biblicists. They believe that the Bible can be trusted as the word of God, it can be relied upon, it's solid rock on which to build.
- They are activists. They have a tradition of social responsibility, always involved in the real world. We will look at that a little more later.
- They are crucicentristic. Crucicentrism means that the cross is at the heart of everything, but it is not a crucifix with Jesus on it, it's a cross that's empty because He's alive and He's risen.

As evangelical Christians, we hold to these distinctives. I want to tell you something about the changing nature of the church. I was asked by the former Prime Minister, John Major, to visit him because he wanted to ask me a question.

He said, 'Why is it that church going is still declining in Britain today after a hundred years, but every single evangelical denomination is growing, and evangelical groups within the other denominations are growing even if the denomination itself isn't growing?'

I said, 'That's easy. People have got enough doubts of their own. They want something to believe in. They want a faith that is personal, a God who comes into their lives and Who makes a difference.' There may be many things wrong with evangelicalism, but confidence in Scripture is not one of them, and a personal relationship with Christ is not another, because on that we stand.

It is a simple fact that, having been 1.8 per cent of the population at the start of the 1970s, depending which statistician you believe, we are now between 5.5 and 7 per cent. Evangelicals have trebled. Take a look at the Church of England. It's a wonderful situation. If you go to an Anglican theological college today, and it's been this way for some years now, over 50 per cent of all the ordinands from Anglican theological colleges this year will be evangelicals. Only a maximum of one third of the Anglican churches in this country are evangelical, so you're getting evangelical clergy placed in non-evangelical parishes. I think that's wonderful, but how much does that mean we need to be praying for our brothers and sisters who are in that position? We need to be praying for those who are going out on the mission field in the depths of darkest Britain.

How much we need to thank God for John Stott and the shout that he raised in the 1950s for two things, that evangelicals might re-engage within the church of England and assume positions of authority. You have had the Bible readings taken this week by a man who served for years as the fourth highest-ranking bishop[2] in this country, and did it as a committed evangelical right along the line. We also ought to be grateful that John Stott pointed out that we've got to get back into the colleges and have evangelical lecturers and students. Not just hiding within conservatism, but moving and taking ground.

My daughter came to me three and a half years ago. She said 'Dad, I want to read theology.'

I said 'Great, I know just the place.'

She said 'And I'm not going there. I've had enough of evangelicals. I want to go to a nice secular university, nice secular context, good general liberal course, then I'll know how to answer for my faith later.'

That's dangerous, but it was great because she did it, and she came out more full of the conviction that Jesus is the only way to God, and that Scripture has the answers, but she also knows how to answer the liberals, because she's gone that route. And things are nowhere near as liberal as they used to be. The theological courses are now very mixed and Vicky found she had some evangelical lecturers. It's a changing church; something is going on.

Many Protestant churchgoers in Britain today are evangelical Christians. We're just coming up to half way. We're going to be the majority voice among Protestants in Britain very, very soon, and we're a pretty united voice. We managed to get three thousand senior church leaders to come to Bournemouth last year to plan an agenda together for the start of a new millennium; Baptists, Pentecostals, Anglicans, Methodist, Salvationists, United Reformed, New Churches, old churches, the lot. That's quite a miracle, because there is an alternative to planning for the future. We could find something we disagree on. If an evangelical in Britain can find another evangelical in Britain with whom they disagree on something important, then we can actually have some fun, because we can discuss the purity of the faith. That will be a great blessing to us all. That's why I wrote all those years ago *With a church like this, who needs Satan?* We love to find where we disagree.

The biggest invitation that we had to disagreement was the rise of the charismatic movement at the beginning of the 1960s. The emphasis of the charismatic movement was on a crisis experience of the Spirit of God in the life of the individual. Some would term it a 'baptism in the Holy Spirit' others a 'filling of the Holy Spirit', others a 'release of the Holy Spirit', different terms but basically a crisis moment, normally accompanied with an opening up to spiritual gifts, healing, prophecy etc, which would include speaking in tongues. This, of course, gave us a real, real, real blessing. Here we could disagree. If you were of charismatic persuasion you could look at those who weren't as being second-class spiritual citizens. If you were not of charismatic persuasion you could look at those who had deserted the word and replaced it with experience.

Who's who?

What they don't understand in America is why, nowadays, we're not quite sure who's who. I'll give you some reasons. Firstly, 43 per cent of evangelicals in this country are charismatic evangelicals. 57 per cent are non-charismatic evangelicals. Those figures are five years old, and if I was guessing, right now it's very close to fifty/fifty. We're not talking about charismatics and evangelicals; we're talking about charismatic evangelicals and non-charismatic evangelicals. What unites them is that they are all evangelicals. For those of us who are of a Reformed disposition, we will be amazed to discover that our Armenian brethren are still evangelicals. For those of us who are Anglicans, we will be amazed to discover that our Baptist friends are still evangelicals, or can be. Charismatic evangelicals and non-charismatic evangelicals are actually beginning to realise more unites them than divides them. They all agree that the Bible is the word of God. They all agree Jesus is the Son of God. They all hold to the traditional doctrines of the church. They all have weaknesses. A non-charismatic evangelical runs the danger of having a head theology, of knowing about God rather than knowing God. A charismatic evangelical runs the danger of a heart theology, of losing touch with allowing Scripture to be the touchstone of all our experience. That little old phrase is so good: 'If you have the word and not the Spirit, you'll dry up; if you have the Spirit and not the word, you'll blow up; but if you have the Spirit and the word together, you'll grow up.' People have discovered that some have not had a crisis experience of the Spirit, they have been progressively sanctified, but they still know the work of the Holy Spirit in their lives. They just went another way. Others have discovered that there are some people who have had a crisis experience of the Spirit in their lives, but have remained relatively normal in the right sense of the word. They don't swing from the chandeliers all the time.

It's incredibly difficult to tell who's who nowadays in Britain. Walk along the line at a Christian convention and the first person's got their arms in the air, the next one's got their hands in their pockets, the next one's half mast, not sure which way to go, the next one's dancing and the last one's hanging onto their songbook for survival. I want to tell you something; they can all love Jesus. They just do it differently. That's a style of worship. If you have an experience of God in your life, don't let the experience of someone else put you down. Do whatever He tells you, go where He leads you, and don't despise the spiritual experience of someone else. We cannot afford the luxury. There's a world out there to win, and our own minor idiosyncrasies should get relegated to the back burner while we go and take this world back for Jesus.

If you want to have a disagreement, there are some things that it's worth disagreeing about. Secondary issues... this is where I get the complaints, always. What's a secondary issue and what's a primary issue? Secondary issues, as defined by the founding council of the Evangelical Alliance in 1846, on which ground I will stand, as none of them are here to defend themselves, include such important issues as paedobaptism. Now you may baptise one way and others of you, along with me, may baptise God's way, but wherever you're at in terms of styles of church government or forms of practice, there are things we are allowed to disagree on, but there are some things we are not allowed to disagree on. Jesus as the Son of God is one of those. The authority of this word is one of those. That's why I believe it is so important that we do not throw out the baby with the bath-water. You will find me conceding very readily that there are sincere people who love the Lord Jesus in the Roman Catholic Church. You will also find me hotly disagreeing with areas of Roman Catholic practice and doctrine, which I believe are contrary to the words of Scripture. What that means is a desire to disagree with dignity and to disagree without being disagreeable, because I don't want to win the argument, I want to commend the truth. Hear me. I don't want to win the argument; I want to commend the truth.

We find the same in areas of ecumenism. We are told that we can work together and that unity is a symbol that will commend the church. I believe it can also be a symbol of confusion. Therefore we should work together as much as we can, and commend each other, but where we cannot do that and confusion is created in people's minds, and there are two or three messages coming over simultaneously we should be very careful to be able to preserve what we know to be truth and to proclaim it.

In the lions' den

It's ever so easy to discuss these things in the hothouse of our local church. I used to have to discuss these things in less pleasant surroundings. Let me describe them to you.

It was a table like this, and it was on the BBC world service. They said, 'Clive, we want you to come and we'd like you to do a series for us, a series of five discussions.'

'Fine' I said.

'Half an hour each' they said.

'Fine' I said.

'We've got five subjects so your researchers will be busy – genetic engineering, homosexuality, the arms race, euthanasia and abortion.'

'How many listeners?'

'We're going to broadcast it three times a week, twenty million each go. You'll get sixty million, each week for five weeks.'

I said 'Done', because if you can't get the gospel over in half an hour, you're pretty bad at it.

Then I said 'Who am I on with?'

'We've got Rafik Abdullah, who is a Muslim barrister, and Rabbi Julia Neuberger representing Judaism. You're the token Christian.'

Oh, it was lovely. Julia always sat opposite me. I always made sure I was opposite her – she's a very tricky lady. She's very able and she's a lovely person. Rafik sat diagonally and then at the end of the table they'd have the guest witness.

It was wonderful, until the week we did homosexuality. This is going to be the single biggest issue in the church in the next two years. It's the big, big issue. Do we have gay clergy or not? Surely Scripture speaks of tolerance and love and accepting people with different dispositions. Surely we have to understand in a modern world that we must be able to reach people, from whatever perspective they come. Even the leader of the Conservative party is now able to send a message of greeting to a Gay Pride rally. So when the homosexuality one came up I thought, 'This is going to be fun, at least I've got a Jew and a Muslim.'

Trevor Barnes, who was presenting it, said 'Our guest lecturer today is doctor Liz Stewart, senior lecturer in theology at the University of South Glamorgan, a committed Roman Catholic, long term Christian, and also in a long term live-in relationship with her lesbian lover.'

Now he always went to Julia first, so he said... 'Clive.'

I said, 'The Scripture is quite straightforward. In seven places in the Bible, Old and New Testament, God says that human relations between people of the same sex are perfectly permissible, friendships are great and should be cultivated, but same sex genital relationships are outside the will and purpose of the living God. It's not what He created us for.'

Trevor said, 'Black and white, no shades of grey?'

I said 'Absolutely none.'

He turned to Julia and said 'What do you think?'

Julia said 'I think Liz has got a right to live in whatever way she wants' – and 90 per cent of Judaism died on the spot.

Then he turned to Rafik, and I thought 'I must be safe here.'

Rafik said 'I agree with Julia, I think Liz should live in the way she wants to.'

That left a very interesting situation: me versus Liz for half an hour, because that was all the programme could do.

I am not sharing this with you this afternoon to get any praise or glory. I am sharing this with you because I want us to understand that we've got two ways of doing this. We can stand on our soap boxes and scream at society, we can shout at a world that disagrees with us, we can be hostile and denounce it, we can have our evangelistic meetings in the safety of our churches and we can speak to the world on our ground, and proclaim the truth, cast our bread upon the waters and go self-satisfied to glory when very little has changed in this country. Or we can actually go in the lions' den and work with the lions, but without compromising on where we're coming from. You may get eaten in the process but that's the fun of it. Please don't get me wrong. I am not saying that it is wrong to hold an evangelistic mission in our churches. There will always be some people who, despite all our personal witness, all our proclamation, all our lifestyle, all the things we've done, all the things we've been, will not be reached with the gospel finally and ultimately until they actually hear the preaching of the word and at that point they will get saved. There's just one or two in that category in every hundred, so let's by all means reach them. But I do want us to get the other ninety-eight first if possible. I believe in preaching missions, totally, and will do them gladly, providing the church recognises they are the end and not the beginning. I went to Billy Graham with Eddie Gibbs and Gavin Reid to ask him to come and do Mission England in 1991 and Billy said 'I will not come and do a mission to save England, but if I can start a snowball rolling down a hill, then I'll come and push the snowball.' That's wonderful. We've got to meet on the world's territory.

Do you want to hear what happened in the World Service programme? Thought you might. Liz said, 'The whole problem with you evangelicals is you're uptight about sex.'

I said, 'Frankly, I thoroughly enjoy it, but I'm perfectly entitled to.'

She said, 'Are you saying your relationship's perfect?'

I said 'No, I abuse my wife, by neglecting her, by being away far too often. I fail to recognise all that she needs, and the person she is, and respect her and bless her as much as I should. I am not saying that my relationship is all that it should be. And besides which, Scripture says that jealousy and selfish ambition come in the same list as same-sex genital relationships, and I certainly practise those first two. But the fact that I am guilty of jealousy and selfish ambition and believe that they have got to come out of my life, does not give you the right to practice same sex genital contact and excuse it on the grounds that I do other things. Because if I believe things are wrong in my life and need to be right, then I believe others should believe that things are wrong in their lives and need to be right as well.'

We went on like this for half an hour, and then dear old Julia intervened, lent across the table and said 'How dare you say, Clive, that Liz has no right to fulfil her God-given inclination?'

'Julia love, you have not been listening. For the last half hour we've been looking at Scripture and how it says quite clearly that same sex genital relationships are outside the will and purpose of God, so how can it be a God-given inclination, Julia? Has God got confused or has He changed His mind?'

Julia said, 'The whole problem, Clive, is you're a nice guy. If you were simply an arrogant bigot, we'd all be far better off.'

At which point, Trevor Barnes said 'I'm sorry, that's all we've got time for. That's the end.'

Love the sinner, hate the sin

Yes, I will have gay people in my home. Yes, I will have them in for interviews and dialogue. Yes, I will share with them, because I believe people need Jesus. I watched my daughter sharing the other day with a lesbian girl. If you do it with a thief, won't you do it with someone with whom you morally disagree? You may say, 'You're compromising.' I'm not compromising. You've never, ever heard me say a word on the media that condones same sex genital relationships, ever. But you have never heard me shout at someone who disagrees with me, because I think we have got to love the sinner and hate the sin. I am appalled by the way the Richard Harries, the Bishop of Oxford, could speak on *Thought for the Day*. Doing radio, I know that the last thing you say is the most important. He did four and a half minutes on the woman caught in adultery and then he said, right at the end, 'and in this Jesus summed up the whole gospel, "therefore neither do I condemn you." Thank you, good morning.' I thought 'Hang on a minute. Jesus also said, "Go and sin no more."' He spoke to the woman, He loved the woman, He cared for the woman, He shared with the woman. He told her that He wasn't condemning her, but she was wrong. Somehow you've got to be able to embrace that and put that together.

But then, in this changing church, there is something else that has to change, and it is our attitude to meetings, because Jesus did not die to give you an abundance of meetings. He died to give you abundance of life. Please, let us meet to study the word of God, please let us meet to pray, please let us meet to encourage and help each other, and please let us do it with an end in view, which is that we might go out and change this world for Jesus. How do we go and change this world for Jesus? By getting involved in this world. In the nineteenth century evangelicals founded leper colonies and staffed them, they changed the hours and conditions of work for women and children by parliamentary legislation. When Bramwell Booth joined with the editor of the *Gazette*, W. T. Stead, they exposed the whole practice of child slavery, children being sold on the continent for child prostitution. William Booth started the first employment exchanges. We worked on issues like cholera and animal rights with Shaftesbury. We did so much, brothers and sisters, we were involved in education, we were involved in medicine, we were involved in prison welfare and prison reform. We were involved in these things and it was evangelical Christians who were at the heart of the campaign against slavery. And it is said of Wilberforce, on his epitaph in Westminster Abbey, 'to all these great and noble attributes he added the eloquent testimony of a Christian life.'

We've got to be involved in changing this world. There are horrendous needs in this world. Three million children in Britain are growing up in poverty today. Two thirds of people sleeping rough in our country today are outside of London. One fifth of all economically active sixteen to nineteen-year-old men were unemployed in 1995. Racism is growing throughout the British isles. Abortions to single women doubled between 1971 and 1991; but please, please, please, let's not just scream 'foul' at society. Let's be involved in making a difference. Let's be running our job creation schemes, our community enterprise projects, let's have our homes for the homeless, let's have our work among the elderly. I'll tell you, the finest opportunities for evangelism in Britain today are probably with the elderly. There are wonderful opportunities that we're not taking because it's not trendy, and yet people who are elderly are lonely, they're struggling to cope. Our demography means that families are shifting and breaking up. There's so much we can do. You heard my cry last night for more older people to be involved in God's world. There is so much that we can do, so much opportunity for the church. You may say 'But that's the social gospel.' Rubbish. Social action without the gospel is little more than sanctified humanism, but the gospel without social action is words without deeds. If we've got a message of life, we ought to be living in the community and changing the lives out there with the gospel: not with it relegated on the back burner, but going out in the name of Christ and changing things by getting our hands dirty. You may say, 'the women's meeting is the best way to do it.' On your hands and knees, getting dirty scrubbing an old lady's floor is the way to do it. It gives you the right to speak Jesus.

The PTA and the Prayer meeting

My wife's a dreadful embarrassment to me. She always has been. I bear the title of evangelist and she's better than I'll ever be. When we moved into South London, she went up to the local school and said to the headmistress 'There's something wrong with this school.'

The head said, 'What's that, Mrs Calver?'

Drawing herself up to her full five foot seven, Ruth said 'We believe in God.'

'Yes', said the head.

'We believe in prayer.'

'Yes', said the head.

Ruth said 'Fine, why don't we have a prayer meeting for the school. Get parents and staff to come together and pray, just once a month. Our home's nearby; it doesn't have to be in a church building.'

If it had been in a church building it would have been the kiss of death, because it would only have been for those people in that church, but 'come to our home, have a meal and we'll pray and then, back into school.'

'No, Mrs Calver', said the head.

Ruth joined the Parent Teachers Association. She got involved in running the PTA disco, the PTA jumble sale and the PTA bazaar. Six months later, she went back to the head and said 'Now, about that prayer meeting?'

It's one thing saying 'No' to a new parent, it's another thing saying 'No' to your best fund-raiser. The head said 'Mrs Calver, you may try.'

Ruth asked people to come together to pray, and a few came together to pray, and they prayed every month, and it went wonderfully until the non-Christians found out. That's always the fun moment, because when the pagans found out, they put in prayer requests to see if it worked. After a sufficiently high ratio of employment being offered to those who were redundant, people being healed, families being reunited, the PTA passed a resolution to make it the PTA prayer meeting. So every year, at the PTA general meeting, after the report on the PTA disco, came the report on the PTA prayer meeting.

One day Ruth came in like the cat that had swallowed the cream, and I knew I was in trouble. I said 'What have you done?'

She said 'A very popular non-Christian has resigned as parent governor and another popular non-Christian is standing. I'm going to stand against her.'

I said 'Darling, this means an election. You'll need a manifesto. I have experience in these things.'

She said 'Your help's the last thing I need.'

I said 'Why's that?'

She said 'Because I'm going to do what you'd tell me I was stupid to do.'

I said 'What's that?'

She said 'I'm going to stand on the basis of the prayer meeting.'

I said 'You're stupid.'

She said, 'Yes, but God's told me and I'm going to do it.'

She was elected on a ratio of three to one, and re-elected eighteen months later on a ratio of four to one. Everything went well until the vicar resigned. He left the area. The problem was he was the Chairman of the Governors. They elected Ruth Chairman of the Governors, and that's when the head resigned. That's when the evangelical Baptist was appointed head. Shortly after a non-Christian was appointed deputy head because there weren't any Christians good enough who applied. Very important, folks, it's a real world out there. We're not a private club. We're going to have to learn to do it well. But I'll tell you what happened to those Governors. There was something new coming through. One of our neighbours saw Ruth putting up the sign for the PTA prayer meeting and said 'Can I come too?' You see, it's amazing what you can do in the five years she had the job of leading the school. She could have gone and started a Christian school, and that may be very commendable in certain situations, and I don't decry anyone who does that, but me? Oh, there's a world out there.

Change the world

I want us to pray for those who go into the political world and change it for Jesus. I want us to pray for those who go into the business world and change it for Jesus. I want us to pray for those who go into the world of education and change it for Jesus. I want to pray for those who go into the world of the trade unions and change it for Jesus. I want to pray for those who move into the inner-city and change it for Jesus, and I want to pray for those who go into the villages: the hardest place to live and work in Britain today as a Christian is in the villages and in the rural churches, it's the hardest mission field. I want to pray for all those who die in the attempt, because there's always cost. Wilberforce worked for forty years before the victory was finally there.

You see there's a world out there and there's a changing church. I think, as I leave these shores, evangelicals have got two options. Option number one, rejoice in what we've done, celebrate, praise God, enjoy our growth, enjoy what we're doing. Option number two: you've barely begun, folks. Go and change this land for Jesus.

A friend of mine is a banker, and he's a wonderful preacher. He said to me one day 'Oh I so want to go and be a preacher. I want to be a vicar or an evangelist.' I said, 'Ken, you're a great preacher, but God's got a lot of vicars and evangelists. He's a bit short of bankers.' Right now, he is the vice-chairman of S.G. Warburgs, the biggest merchant bankers in Britain. We've got to go and be people for Jesus in a church for Jesus, a church that's involved in the community, changing it, a church that's relevant in society, doing something for it, a church that abandons the church magazine and makes it the local community freebie newspaper, gets the gospel through. We've got to be a church that goes out into the community, a church where we are blessing and encouraging those with special gifts and ministries, those working with the prisoners. What is going on in Lewes prison, it's fantastic: those who are working with the addicts, those who are working with the homeless. Brothers and sisters, you've got enough to keep you going for years, but you're in a changing situation. I'm going to a nation where we're going down. You're going up.

Something has started in this nation. Don't stop. Something has happened in our evangelism. Don't stop. Something has happened as we try and get involved in the media and the real world. Don't stop. Something has happened as we really try to get involved in changing our communities and reaching our neighbours. Don't stop. Don't go back to tearing each other apart. Join together, love each other, forgive each others' faults. Go and get this world back for Jesus. Pray for those of us who've got other mission fields to go to. And don't stop.

---

[1] Bebbington, D.W., *Evangelicalism in Modern Britain: A History from the 1730s to the 1980s*, (London: Unwin Hyman, 1989)

[2] Baughen, Bishop Michael. The Bible readings were publishing in *A Voice in the Wilderness, Keswick Ministry 1997,* (Carlisle: Paternoster Press, 1997)

The State of the Nation and The State of the Church

by Roy McCloughry – 1997

ROY McCLOUGHRY

Roy is Director of Kingdom Trust, a consultancy on applied social ethics. Formerly an economist, Roy became Director of the Shaftesbury Project after leaving the London School of Economics. He was John Stott's first Study Assistant and now writes, researches and speaks on Christian approaches to social, economic and political issues. He has written twelve books; among them his bestseller *Men and Masculinity*. *Belief in Politics,* a collection of interviews with leading politicians, set off a national debate about the moral and spiritual beliefs of political leaders before the 1997 election. He is Chairman of *Third Way* magazine and a Director of Lion Publishing. He travels widely speaking and lecturing and makes programmes for BBC television.

The State of the Nation

Introduction

It's important for us to engage with the culture we live in. God's word we call 'truth unchanging' but the culture around us is changing. The needs of people are expressed in different ways, the blind spots are in different areas of our lives. The things which we think of as evil come somewhere else in the list of all possible evils, and things which a previous generation thought of as good are now seen as compromises. We live in a perplexing and fast-changing world, where the rapid pace of change dislocates one generation from another. The assumption of the newest generation is that, because of the rapid pace of change, the wisdom of the previous generation is not applicable. It is this rapid pace of change that leads ultimately to the generation gulf. In a world which desperately needs the older generation to mentor and befriend a bewildered younger generation, how are we then to understand this world that we live in?

I want to talk about five tensions that exist in our world, which are important for us to understand if we want to engage with it effectively. I'm convinced that many people I talk to, in the media or politics or wherever, just don't understand what the church is saying. They genuinely cannot hear it. Many of them say they don't believe the church has got any message. Why, what kind of world do they live in? How do they see things? I want to start by asking you how you think of the various worlds that we have lived in as a civilisation. I don't want to go right back to Egypt and to the Old Testament, maybe just as far back as the medieval world. And I like to think of the different worlds we live in as games. I think of the medieval world as the game of chess; everything in its place, its strata; the pawns, bishops, knights, kings, queens, rooks – all with their separate moves, all about strategy and power.

What kind of a world do we live in?

When I think of the modern world, I think of the game of
Monopoly; progress through accumulation, and a little bit of ruthless-
ness as well. Many of us have been brought up in the modern world,
in which to progress through life is to end it with a whole bundle of
things, status and titles. But we are moving on from the modern
world. Generations to come will look back at the modern world, like
we look at the medieval world, and they'll have a different name to
call themselves by.

We're a culture in transition between the modern world and the
world that is coming, which many of your sons and daughters are
already living in. We haven't given a name to that world yet, and so it's
called 'after' modern or post-modern, because when you put 'post' in
front of something, it means after. It's a world of media and entertainment, of uncertainty, where people are not sure who they are, where
one million people are in therapy at any one time in this country.
What kind of game do we call the post-modern world? I think we
call it the lottery, where superstition rules, and people are desperate to
get somewhere in life without paying any cost except £1 for the
ticket. It was summed up in a quote from Clifford Longley recently;
'Western civilisation suffers from a strong sense of moral and spiritual exhaustion. Having constructed a society of unprecedented
sophistication, convenience and prosperity, nobody can remember
what it was supposed to be for.'

Our job in mission is to make Christ visible for a world to whom He
is invisible. That is the essence of mission. We may we think we live in comfortable times, but all you've got to do is change the tangent of which you
come on our century to be shocked. For ours has been the bloodiest
century of all; more people have been killed by war in this modern sophisticated century than in the five thousand years before combined. Our
world is cruel, violent and bloody. It is a world in which, in the 1980s, 8
per cent of the rain forest, the lungs of the planet, disappeared. An area
three times the size of France, just gone and not renewable.

Many of you have been brought up with natural uncertainty;
earthquakes and whirlwinds and volcanoes, things that were more

powerful than you were; natural uncertainties. But your grandchildren live with manufactured uncertainty, for we have changed the world that we live in. The things that are a threat to the world now – the acid rain, the desertification, the global warming, the things that are a sword of Damocles over the future of our planet – have been made by us. They are the costs of industrialisation, of consumption. Does our world have a future? You don't have to be a Christian prophet to say it has an uncertain future. So this generation is facing things that no other generation had to deal with before. We literally do not know what will happen next.

In the context, then, of this uncertainty at the end of the millennium, how do we approach our culture? It is very important to do this, and one of the reasons is summed up in that little proverb, a fish discovers water last. Because a fish breathes the water all the time, it's not aware of the water, just as some of the things that are most close to us are most invisible to us. Some of the things that have most power over us are the things we take for granted. It's true sometimes of us in the church, as it is of people outside the church. So it's important for us to make our culture visible in order that we might be able to address it effectively, to engage with it, and to conduct effective mission to it.

Modern to post-modern

There are five tensions in this world that is on the move, and I've already mentioned one of them: from the modern world to the post-modern world. The modern world, the world that we're aware of around us, came out of the last two hundred years: out of the rise of science, the rise of the idea of the individual and the sense of confidence that we had come of age, that we had arrived. We no longer needed a reference point in God that gave meaning to the world, we were our own self reference point. It is this modern world which has given birth to so many great inventions and ideas. The cleverness of the human race has been amazing but the violence and the environmental decay have been a high cost. And the highest cost of all has been the removal of that sacred canopy over the whole of life represented by the worship of God. No longer does everything in life refer to God as it did maybe in the medieval times, where a debate on the rate of interest was a debate about theology. Now religion is an optional extra, a marginal activity for those who prefer to go to church rather than to play golf on Sunday.

The modern world was a world of confidence; we can do it! If there's a disease, we can provide the cure; if there's a disaster we can rebuild; there's nothing that we cannot do on our own. But this modern world has given rise to all the horrors that have beset us and since the First World War, in particular, there has been increasing uncertainty about whether it's been worth it, and a pessimism, a lack of confidence and a belief that the modern world has let us down. In young people today it's seen in irony and satire, a sense in which the authority of scientists, theologians and philosophers is called to account, and their authority is not recognised. Those who have built the modern world are seen to have borrowed resources from the next generation and to have let this generation down. There is a tension for those of us who still live in the confidence and optimism of the modern world; building structures, not knowing what they're there for, finding cures but finding problems as a result of the very advances we make.

Global and local

The second tension is between the global and the local. The state of the nation is almost an old-fashioned concept, because the nation as an idea is disappearing. The nation is given its identity by the bound-aries around it, and it says, within these boundaries we are British or Welsh or French or whatever. But we live now in a global world in which the media, the movement of trade, tourism and the fast flowing markets of stocks and shares and capital around the world are connecting it up, so that we are an inter-connected world. This means you may be driving a car made on the other side of the world but which has a familiar British badge on it. You can buy exotic produce formerly only obtainable in season, so seasons have lost their meaning as far as cooking is concerned.

In the next ten years you will be able to phone Japan for the price of a local call. The whole world will open up in telecommunications.

I can work on my computer here in my room at Keswick, and plug into the phone socket and work on a computer in Peru, as if I were sitting at the computer myself. I can speak to people via a video camera and see them on the screen, who are in Australia. I typed in the name of a medicinal drug on my computer, and one hundred articles came up on my screen. The information society is connecting us all over the world. The problem won't be a lack of information, but the global world has a sting in its tail because it says this: all cultures are equal. That is the price of what is called globalisation. There is no argument for being a superior culture, whether it is China or Russia or Europe or whatever: all cultures now are considered equal. And if all cultures are considered equal, the sting in the tail is that all gods are considered equal.

If you read Norman Davies' wonderful new book on Europe, ask yourself the question – what was it that gave Europe its identity? It was Christianity. Yet we live in a world in which to claim any superior authority for one culture or one faith is deeply offensive. All cultures now are mixed. The McDonaldisation of the world has progressed, so that you can walk through a Cairo slum and see Coca Cola signs swinging in the breeze. It's been more effective sometimes than Christian mission. And all cultures are mixing up. We've got access to all kinds of things so that we are a mixed culture, and some of us are mourning the death of English culture. John Redwood says, 'the politics of tomorrow is the politics of identity.' I think in that at least he is right: we are people who feel that we are losing a sense of identity. One of the reasons for many of the tragic wars around the world is this loss of identity: culture has been eroded, people are feeling insecure and they are reverting back to the old tribal patterns.

If you ask what was wrong in Bosnia-Herzegovina where the artificial country of Yugoslavia broke up, it was that people could not accept the artificiality of the compromises that had been put upon them for so many years, and they went back to the old tribal conflicts. Something similar happened in Rwanda. All over the world there are new tensions: the old wounds are opening up, because people are looking for a sense of identity.

There are good things in globalisation. There's tremendous choice in the supermarket, in the goods that we can buy. There's tremendous freedom to travel the world and see it, but there is confusion. One of the great philosophers of international relations in Harvard University looks ahead and says, 'What will be the cause of major war in the twenty-first century? It will be the clash of civilisations.' We have great power blocks which are no longer represented by political ideology. The left/right divide is over. What is more important in the world that is coming are the clashes of religious ideology: the clashes of the great secular civilisations of China and Russia; the great clashes between Islam, Judaism and Christianity. These are the fault lines of the twenty-first century. The generations that come will have to deal with them, and if peace is to come and the world is not to become again a place of religious violence, then we need people who understand the world's civilisations and the world's religions, and do not hide from them.

China will have the biggest economy by the year 2020. The league table in the year 2020 will go like this: top five economies in the world – China, US, Japan, India and Indonesia. Those of us brought up thinking of India as a poor country, to which aid should be sent, will be amazed to find that by 2020 it will become a major industrial power. The world is changing. The days of the 'West and the rest' are over. We thought we were developed, and described the rest of the world as 'developing' – catching up with us. But many people in the world are not bothering to catch up with us. Japan is a modern society but it has no Christian base. Many societies, which are passing us in terms of economic and political power, have philosophies driving them which are foreign to our way of thinking. We need to understand them. Let me give you one measure of the rapid pace of change: in 1962, South Korea had an income per head like the Sudan. It was that far behind. Now South Korea rivals the richest countries in Europe.

The change that has happened in the last thirty-five years has been enormous. Commentators say that the twenty-first century will be Asian, not European. And our great need is to understand Asian culture, because just as we colonised the world with Coca Cola and

McDonalds, so Asia will colonise the world with its own concepts, and we desperately need people like Vinoth Ramachandra in Sri Lanka who understand the relationship between Christianity and Hinduism – or Buddhism, the culture of the east. When I went to Africa, I was amazed to learn that the average age of Kenya was fourteen. The average age of people in this country is around forty-three. Our culture is often middle-aged. We have a greying population, but in Kenya, most of the people are adolescent, and it has the energy, the enthusiasm and the problems of a teenage culture.

There is a tension between the global and the local. Some of us feel threatened by this massive expansion, and we're trying to build walls round the local, to find a new identity, and yet we need people who can understand the world as an entirety, because we are so connected.

Tradition and choice

We live in a post-traditional society. That's not a society where tradition has disappeared, but a society in which its place has changed. Many of you will have been brought up in a traditional society, where your place in life, the kind of person you would marry, the kind of job you would do, maybe were more given than they are now. There are still cultures in the world where your tradition takes a lot of the strain of making choices. But our society is based on a very special kind of freedom, a freedom measured by choice. The more choices you have in our world, the more free you are said to be. We have the phrase from the Thatcher period – free to choose. I want to talk a bit about consumerism in a moment, but I believe that too much choice can lead to anxiety.

We live in a world in which one million people are in some kind of therapy or analysis today. The person sitting in the pew in 1997 feels a sense of inadequacy. In the Victorian era you would rail at them with judgement, trying to temper their ego and their rebellion with the knowledge of the power and the holiness of God. We still need the power and the holiness of God, but many people today are on a search for the self: they feel inadequate, they have nothing to contribute; they feel powerless with respect to the problems of the world. When they are told that they are sinners, which they are, they add it to the list of their own burdens, and go away, sometimes not knowing of the saving power of Christ. Our society needs the preaching of the love of God like no other society has done; to understand the love and the mercy and the salvation of God for themselves, because we are an anxious society.

I was here with the BBC a couple of weeks ago, filming Long Meg and her daughters, a circle of stones. I was doing some meditations for a programme. There were lots of people sitting in the circle, doing rituals, in a kind of covert way. Behind one of the stones we found a binding of different coloured wools which had obviously been used in some symbolic ritual. We are a superstitious, anxious society: wanting to find our place but not knowing what it could be. The freedom of choice that we have has brought anxiety and not freedom. The Christian faith says that there is something, which previous people have discovered, which is relevant to you today – the opposite of the idea that rapid change dislocates the world. The things that matter have been discovered in Christ and portrayed in the Bible and passed down as received wisdom, from generation to generation, so the elderly of today have got something to tell young people. People do not accept tradition in the way that they did – unquestioning because it has been proved true by a previous generation – tradition has become another choice. I can choose to be traditional, as one of the many choices I have.

There is a problem: in this world of uncertainty, in which anything goes, in which morality has become a lifestyle issue, there is a new and ominous search for power and dogmatism. The thing which I fear more than anything for my children in the twenty-first century is the rise of fundamentalism. By this I do not mean the word which many of us will hold as precious, which is the taking of the Bible seriously. I mean a dogmatic conviction that I am right, and that you are wrong; that the truth that I have is so true and so unpolluted that it gives me the right to ignore what you believe: I do not have to be open to dialogue. If I evangelise, I do not have to listen to those who are talking to me, because I have the truth and they do not. This kind of fundamentalism, which is brewing in every religion of the world, is a reaction against the breakdown of authority in our society. It's a reaction against the liberalism and the consumerism of our day which says anything goes, as long as you feel fulfilled – anything goes. It is an attempt to bring back authority and order to our world. But the road it leads down is the road to violence. If I am right and you are wrong, it is a short hop to say I am good and you are evil, and it is a shorter hop when that is said, to saying that I must survive and you must be destroyed. An American rabbi said recently in *Time* magazine: 'suddenly it's almost sexy to be a religious fundamentalist.' I am a Christian, I'll be a Christian all my life, but I have no right to impose my views on other people. I have the right to persuade them as they have the right to persuade me. I have the right to preach and worship freely but I have no right to impose or manipulate or exploit.

Politically, we live in a democracy, and there's a very good set of Christian reasons why democracy is sometimes a good kind of society to live in. You know, Winston Churchill's old proverb that it's the worst form of government except all the others that have ever been tried. Richard Neuhaus, the American thinker, said once that: 'Democracy's the appropriate kind of society, the appropriate kind of government, in a fallen world in which nobody, including the church, can infallibly speak for God.' It's an expression of humility in which all persons and all institutions are held accountable to what he calls 'transcendent purposes imperfectly discerned.' Of course it's unsatisfactory. Only the kingdom of God is satisfactory. We grumble about it. But the very discontent we have is a sign of a healthy society. We are free to criticise our politicians, hold them to account: to say this isn't the kind of world I want to live in. We know that there is one world coming, in which we'll be fulfilled, in which righteousness and justice will prevail. A longing and a hunger for the kingdom of God is dangerously misplaced when we try to create it for ourselves in this world. History shows us that when Christians, instead of pointing to the kingdom of God that is coming and is perceived by faith in Christ, try to build it out of political building blocks, it can quickly lead to either fascism or communism. There is no such thing as a perfect world, before the reign of Christ in the new world. We live in tension – between the already and the not yet – of the kingdom of

God, in a history which witnesses to compromise, to the fact that we as the church are growing the wheat and the tares together, and the world itself is a deeply compromised world with both good and bad in it. And yet there are those who are so frustrated with the things that they disagree with in this world that they will impose their view on the rest, rather than serve them with the love of Christ.

The way of Christ is the way of the cross, not the way of triumphalism. There is a problem because the things we value have given way to a chaotic false freedom of choices which promise so much liberation to people, whether it's a sexual or technological freedom, and deliver so much bondage. Be careful. Don't let your frustration lead you away from the cross, or give you rights that you do not have to impose your world view on others whom you think of as lesser than yourselves. There is no such way. It is folly to believe it. That way is the way of violence.

Truth and power

The very truths that we believed in have been eroded. We live in a religiously plural world. I was doing my piece to camera in Long Meg and her daughters, talking about the growth of paganism and witchcraft in our society. A recent report says that there are over two hundred and fifty thousand pagans and witches in our society. I did it about thirteen times, because I forgot what I was saying – I had to go back and start again. There were some people by one of the stones. I was speaking loudly, and one of these guys came up to me and said 'What are you doing? I can hear what you're saying.' 'Oh,' I said, 'we're making a television programme about Long Meg and her daughters.' 'Are you just covering the sacred sites?' he said. I said, 'We've done Hadrian's wall as well.' He looked at me quite threateningly actually, and walked away very slowly. For this was a sacred site. For me it is a site which celebrates dark powers – nothing to do with holiness. But for him, as a New Ager, it's a sacred site.

Everybody's into spirituality; it's the new word at parties. If you want to talk your head off at a party, you can talk about spirituality till the cows come home. All spiritualities in our world have become equal. Somebody is into astrology; another is into crystals; another is into psycho-kinesis, or whatever it is; the list goes on and on. All these things are worthy of respect, we are told, in the New Age. We are told that tolerance is the greatest virtue in our society but tolerance is only a virtue in a society in which people have commitments and the post-modern world has no commitments. It is because I am a Christian and I believe that Christianity is true and that Christ is God, that my tolerance means something. But if I believe that what I believe is no more important and true than anybody else's beliefs, then it's not tolerance – it's indifference.

Our society is at its most vitriolic where Christians claim not just that Christ – or Christianity – is true, but it is the truth by which all other claims to truth are judged. In our society that is the most offensive thing that you can claim, especially with liberal people. For instance, you'll be invited to dinner by people who are not Christians, and they will ask you to say grace, often, before the meal! And there is you, thinking what an opportunity to witness for God. In my grace I shall give them the gospel. But what are they doing? They're saying, this is your truth, we would like to be polite, and gracious, and recognise that we are decent people, we're not intolerant people, we know that you are a Christian, and we know that Christians say grace; so we'd like you to say grace because you might feel more comfortable. But it's your truth; it's not our truth.

In our day there's no such thing as 'the truth' anymore. There is your truth, and there is my truth, but there is no longer the truth. Truth is not universal in the post-modern world; it is local. You hear young people saying, Christianity is only spreading all over the world because it went with the power of Europe; it went with the colonialisation of Europe; it should have remained a local story. But because it robed the power of trade, a political colonisation, it has spread outside its limits. You hear in sociology courses round the world the fact that the big stories have let us down. The big stories of communism, feminism, Christianity, anything that starts off 'the meaning of life is…' is no longer true by definition. There is only your truth and my truth and they are equal with one another.

The second thing about this is that truth and power are seen together. If I make a claim to my view of the Christian faith being true for everybody, as I do, because I believe Jesus Christ is Lord of all creation, that is seen to be a bid for power over people. All truth claims are seen as power bids. This is difficult for us as Christians, and if it continues, will make Christian witness a very important but difficult thing. Because all views are equal in the world in which we live, because nobody's got any claim to superiority, because tolerance has become an empty virtue, then to claim that Christianity's true for everybody, that Christ came to save the world, is seen as a bid for power over people who don't believe it. So Christianity is held up to suspicion.

People, younger people in particular, are suspicious of claims. Be careful what you claim, because people are looking for the evidence. It's very easy on a platform in a meeting to make claims for the Christian faith. God's plan is good for God, it may not be good for you and for me, our life may be a life of suffering. Let's not turn the gospel into a public relations exercise for the Christian faith. Our claims are under the spotlight. Tony Thistleton, Professor of Theology at Nottingham, one of the most eminent theologians in our country, says that Christian love must be non-manipulative love. If our methods as Christians are suspect, we live in a world that will find us out. If we claim great healings on a platform somewhere, that are claimed during the meeting for their spectacular nature but cannot be verified afterwards, then we are under suspicion of manipulating people.

The world we live in, by its confusion, its problems with truth and its suspicion of power, brings us to the heart of the cross itself. The things which we need to display are the servanthood of Christ and the life of the cross. Tony Thistleton says this:

> The claims to truth put forward in Christian theology ... call for love where there is conflict, for service where there are power interests, and for trust where there is suspicion. In a world where there is no trust we need to build it. In a world where messages are based on their bid for power, we need to give up power and become the servants of others. In a world where conflict and power interests collide, we need to love our enemies.

In other words, we are under pressure, from a society that frankly disbelieves us, to live the gospel. What the world is looking for are not great claims, not wonderful excitement, but authentic Christlikeness. The people we are going to with the gospel are described by Sigmund Baumann, the great Oxford philosopher, in these words: 'They are vagabonds and tourists.' He says this

> What keeps them on the move is disillusionment with the place of the last sojourn, and the forever smouldering hope that the next place that he's not visited yet, perhaps the place after the next, may be free from faults which repulsed him in the places he's already tasted. Pulled forward by hope untested, pushed from behind by hope frustrated, the vagabond is a pilgrim without a destination, a nomad without an itinerary.

People are going from one thing to another to give life meaning. This week it's the diet that's going to take three stone off them and make them beautiful, next week, it's the vibrating crystal in which the powers of the age will tell them what to do; the week after it's the astrology column: they are on a search for meaning and identity and purpose, in which they are vagabonds searching in the dustbins of life.

We need as never before to bring the truth of Jesus Christ, as lived out in the people of God. Doctrine is not enough; words are not enough for this generation. They are suspicious of words; they've had it with ideology. What they want is to see the distinctiveness of a life that is not based on bids for power, that does not get its identity from conflict, which is truthworthy and has integrity and reminds them of the person of Christ.

Consumption and meaning

The last tension which I've got no time to go into is the tension between consumption and meaning. Meaning has been divorced from messages and is now attached to things. The job of the advertising and marketing industry is to attach meaning that belongs to the spiritual journey to a pair of jeans: to say if you buy this you can be a changed person – you can go from being this unlovely person to being this accepted beautiful person. In this world, having has replaced being as a mode of identity. In this world what my grandfather called debt is called credit; and he would be told he was foolish to wait five years to get married, to save, so he could pay for what he owned, because now he can just put it on his credit card. Access takes the waiting out of wanting. This is a world in which we're very uncertain about tomorrow – we want it now; give it to me now, I'll pay for it later. This is a world where, when we face the final frontier (to follow a Star Trek analogy) of death, we find ourselves deluded with all our things that we cannot take with us.

This is a mapping exercise of the culture we live in. It's so difficult to understand this fast moving culture, to be prophetic in a way that is effective and accurate, but I want to encourage you to say that if we can understand the world, if we can listen and be humble and open and yet committed to Christ, there are still people out there who are hungry for the word of God. Don't be discouraged, there is good soil out there for your words to fall on. Often the people who are hungry do not understand what we are saying, because for them the map of the world is different to the map forty or fifty years ago. So as we go to them, in our humility let's remember to listen as well as to speak, so that in understanding the signs of the times, we might bring them a message about the Lord who is king of our times.

The State of the Church

Religious faith is the conviction of things not seen. I want to say several things about this for a start, because we are tempted most to build institutions out of faith, and as soon as we do, we are tempted away from religious faith as the conviction of things not seen, to maintain and tinker with the institutions that we have made. One of those distressing things I find today in the evangelical movement is people talking about church rather than talking about God. Religious faith has got as its premise the idea that God is invisible, and the gift of a good God to the world is the freedom of God's creation. If God was visible we could not be free because, as many of the Old Testament prophets found out, we cannot bear the holiness of God. It is in the goodness of God's mercy that God is invisible to us. The invisibility of God, which means that we have to believe in God by faith, is a sign that one of the most basic things to the whole of creation is the idea of freedom. God's retreat in terms of invisibility – though His presence is always with us – is a sign that He wants us to be free.

Coherence

God is not coercive. People who say 'I wish that God would write it in the sky' could not be more wrong! God does not do anything to force His creation to believe in Him. What God wanted was for people to worship Him freely. He constantly interacts with the world, he sustains every part of it. But it is this coherence throughout the whole of creation, the fact that it is understandable, that makes scientific investigation possible. Science is becoming more taken up with chaos, and one of the reasons for that is that as science loses its roots in a Christian understanding of the world and the coherence of the world that the Creator has given it, it begins not to understand the world.

It's a coherent world. Nor has science succeeded in disproving Christianity, much as many have attempted it. In the United States, over 39 per cent of scientists say they believe in a personal God. In 1916 that figure was 42.8 per cent, not a major shift over the most intense period of scientific investigation.

Ambivalence

God also acts in the world so that every action is capable of other explanations, but each action is an invitation to faith. It's to do with freedom again. God is concerned that we respond to Him and His works because we believe in Him, but in every action that God does, there is the possibility of walking away from it with another explanation. Even when Jesus did miracles, they were not coercive. There were those who did not believe. Jesus says about the generations such as ours: 'Blessed are those who do not see, and yet believe.' We walk by faith and not by sight.

Resurrection

This faith that we have in an invisible God Who sustains the whole world, and acts in it all the time, but Whose actions can be given all kinds of alternative explanations, because He desires us to be free, is not just my subjective opinion, but is predicated on our response to one event in human history; the resurrection of Jesus Christ. This is an activity of God in history, the greatest event of all human history, on which human history revolves, which itself is capable of all kinds of other explanations, misinterpretations and distortions. But it is a unique event on which Christianity depends for its very life and its future. 50 per cent of people in Britain say they believe in the resurrection, but do they understand the implications of the resurrection? Paul states this importance very baldly when he says, 'No resurrection, no Christianity'. For the last two thousand years Christians have lived and died in the name of Jesus Christ.

Religion has been a mixed bag. Our generation has come to see it as a mixed bag. Many of my friends who are not Christians would not come to church because they believe it to be unjust. The treatment of women in the church has been a major stumbling block for them. They would not go to church because they see it as perpetrating injustice. The one thing everyone has to deal with is the persistence of religion in a world which is increasingly fed up with the sterility of the mechanistic and the materialistic. One of the reasons for the wave of New Ageism is that people cannot live by secularisation alone. People are hungry and searching for meaning and for spirituality.

Response

Faith is the response to the evidence of God's presence. I find it very difficult to believe that people can look at the world of creation, and think that behind this world is chance or coincidence. Faith is not just an individual response, but it's also the foundation of a new community, historically and geographically. When people say to me, as they do in a pluralistic society, 'What right have you to say that about God?', I say, 'I'm sorry, but these are not my views, these are the views of a whole tradition of two thousand years of people, from every tribe and nation. I stand in the middle of a tradition. These are views I came into. I am not on my own, I am part of a cosmic community, which stretches back in history and across geographically.'

I'm part of an ongoing story which gives my life purpose and meaning. In an essay entitled 'Where Religion Meets Politics', Professor of Politics at Hull University P. K. Perec says this: 'When the main concern is to get on in life, to pursue pleasure and to promote self interest, there is a tendency to cut moral corners and to bend moral principle to the requirements of personal convenience. Religion stresses the quality of the human soul and forces people to examine what kind of human beings they have become.' I think that's true. In a world where convenience is one of the dominant moralities of our day – or amoralities of our day – and things are bent to our convenience, what religion does is to force us to examine the human condition honestly. That doesn't mean that we accept anything that calls itself religious. Our world is religiously plural; not really secular. We need wisdom and discernment about what is good and what is bad. He continues in this article, 'although religion has been a force for evil, it has also been a force for good, generating a kind of energy, commitment, passion and willingness to suffer, that was sometimes lacking in wholly secular motivations.' He is not, as far as I know, a Christian, but that kind of comment is becoming more prevalent today. People are beginning to see that religion is important. There is a kind of sacrifice, a commitment, a passion for justice, a concern with truth, that people who are religious have, that the secular world often does not have.

Church attendance

In Britain, 12 per cent of the population go to church once a week or more, compared to 19 per cent in other countries, 40 per cent in the U.S. So in terms of church attendance we're quite low. 11 per cent of people read the Bible every day, and as many as 44 per cent pray daily. If I could give you another lecture, I would talk about the importance of prayer to evangelism. It is often seen as coercive today to knock on a door and evangelise somebody. It is not seen as coercive to offer to pray with somebody. The willingness of local congregations to say that they are praying for the needs of the community, to have a box where people can anonymously put their needs in, is still seen as supportive, and is something we should think about in our mission strategy.

In the world there are 1.9 billion Christians: 34 per cent of the world are Christians. 54 per cent of these are Roman Catholics. The church grows by one hundred thousand every day, one third of whom are children. The church is growing faster than the world population – 1.8 to 1.6 per cent per annum respectively. While the church grows world-wide, and new churches are being added, one of the most important things to understand about our culture is that there is more believing than belonging. 61 per cent of the British population say they believe in God. We are not a secular society. 50 per cent say they believe in heaven; 37 per cent in miracles; 25 per cent in angels; 20 per cent in hell and the devil. 37 per cent believe that God is concerned personally with individuals. 68 per cent of the British people consider themselves Christians, 71 per cent of these believe in the resurrection – these are high figures. Grace Davie, a sociologist, who has written very effectively on Christianity in Britain, says this about the phenomenon of believing without belonging:

> Religious belief, when not associated with active membership of a church, tends to be associated with superstitious belief, while church attendance tends to be antithetical (that is against) superstition. Moreover, we have some evidence that for those people who do not go to church, yet say they are religious and pray often, religious belief has moved quite far from the orthodox church position and is really much closer to what would normally be called superstition.

In other words, church membership seems to be vital for giving content to one's faith, for making it coherent and understandable.

Believing without belonging

We seem to be a religious society. Where are all these people who believe these things? Because they are not getting the kind of teaching that you are blessed with here at Keswick, the distortions accumulate, and what is religious belief becomes superstitious belief. Believing and belonging are part of the same Christian faith. It is not a faith that is based on individualism; it is a faith which says we need each other. It is as the community of Jesus Christ that we walk forward. Love is not a word that can be demonstrated in an individualistic way. Christianity is a faith of the community, as much as a faith of the individual.

The basic building block of our creation is of the person in community. The only thing that was not good, before the introduction of evil into the world, was man alone. God said 'It is not good for man to be alone'. Why? Because this individualised person could not reflect the God who is Trinity. God is person in community and, made in the image of God, we are person in community. Being in community is essential to being human, which is why the fact that one in three of the population in the next twenty years will live on their own is a tragedy for our society. And it is why those of us who are involved in social action and social justice do so on strong theological grounds; because we believe in a Trinitarian God who is person in community.

Believing and belonging are part of the same faith, because God wanted a community who would freely and voluntarily worship Him. And at the end of time, this cross-cultural community is described as being from every tribe and nation. Christianity is not just about some individual search for inner meaning, but is focused in two places. Firstly, the inward journey is not focused on the self but on God. Contemplation and meditation are not introversion and introspection, but meditation on the person of a holy God. Self identity is a gift to the person who is willing to make the worship of God and obedience to God the stuff of their inner life. The inward journey is focused on God – but the new outwardness is not based on self interest but on others and the needs of others. The Christian is given the motivation for this outward journey in mission and service and a passion for justice because of their discovery that life is a gift in which we realise that we are loved by God. Our response and our responsibility is to demonstrate this to others, so Christian spirituality and social justice are both based on a response and an expression of the love of God to us as we are now.

Social justice

Many Christians today are involved in social action, demonstrating that Christians worship a God of justice, and must come to terms with the fact that in worship we become what we worship. If we believe we worship a God of justice, we must become the people of justice. The revelation of God becomes the requirements of His people, because we are in a covenant relationship with God. If Israel was a light to the Gentiles, and the church is a light to the nations, part of the light of God is that the holiness of God is exemplified in His righteousness and His justice. How can Christians in a fallen and unjust world not be concerned about issues of justice?

Here is Yasmin Alibhai Brown, a Moslem writer, talking about Christianity:

For the first time, I can think about Christianity in its original form, the good Samaritan faith. With the end of the British Empire, and the declining power of the church in Britain, Christianity is far less attached to politics in a traditional sense. Take the reaction of the churches to the new asylum law. The churches have done more than anyone else to fight these iniquitous laws; the Jewish community and some black groups have opposed these laws, but many ethnic minority groups have done nothing. Across Europe, most so-called radicals have failed to confront attempts to reduce asylum rights in the way that Christian groups have. I'm incredibly impressed by that.

Here is a person who is a Muslim, impressed by the passion for justice that Christian groups have had, on behalf of others, who are falling foul of unjust laws in Britain on asylum. This is one instance of how Christian social action can do things to move people.

Some of you might have heard of the think-tank, Demos, one of the most innovative think-tanks in our country. In an article on religion in its journal, Ben Jupp, who is senior researcher at Demos says this

> Much of the best innovation in the provision of local health, homelessness, community regeneration, and drug-related services is now being shaped by people with strong religious beliefs. Projects such as the Marylebone health centre, the Kaleidoscope drugs project in Kingston, Surrey, and the Bromley by Bow community centre in east London have been pioneers in taking account of the full range of human needs, when providing care. This resurgence of religious engagement with the wider community has coincided with withdrawal of the state from direct provision of many services.

As far as I know he is not a Christian, he's writing as a secular commentator. I was absolutely amazed at the way he so positively portrayed the engagement of Christianity with the modern world.

In Christianity the quest for social justice is the other side of, and the inevitable companion of, the quest for true spirituality. The God we worship is a God of justice as well as love, and God wants a world that is more rather than less just. At the age of fourteen, I was under a lot of pressure. I thought I was losing my faith, and I picked up *Strength to Love* by Martin Luther King. I read it and it changed my life. Here was a person who wasn't just concerned with his own personal insurance policy for eternity; not concerned just about the ghetto, and staying in the comfort zone of the Christian church, but a man who thought the Christian faith was worth risking your life for. A man who knew that the God he worshipped was a God of justice, and wherever he came against injustice he had to take a risk, to be against injustice.

The kingdom of God

One of the ways we focus on this set of tensions between the inner and the outer life is to look at the kingdom of God. One of the central motifs of the New Testament and, in fact, the Old Testament is the reign of God. What kind of world does the reign of God consist of? The reign of God means that there is another way of living in this world; we don't have to live for money or power, to build empires. We can live in this world as if there's another agenda: as the book of Acts tells us, 'these worship another king, one Jesus.' This kingdom is currently invisible, as is its king. The life of this kingdom can only be lived by faith, but the teaching of Jesus left His followers in no doubt about how a life lived like this was to be lived. The parables, the miracles, the life of Christ, were evidence of the presence of the kingdom among us, and a guide to it.

Graham Cray, principal of Ridley College, Cambridge, says these things about the kingdom

> The sick are given back the possibility of an active role in society; the demonised are set free and restored to normal relationships. Cleansed lepers can come back into the community. Those experiencing untimely bereavement have their loved ones and bread-winners restored. Jesus' table fellowship of tax collectors and sinners was a foretaste of their place in the messianic banquet of the last day; His acceptance of women and little children gave them a special or best part in the kingdom both present and future.

To live in this way, to see our job as restoring people to community through the work of Christ, is a difficult road to go on: no promise of the avoidance of suffering, tragedy and failure, and high standards to live up to. Only in the next world will we live in a world where, by nature, we please God. We live now in a world of disease, evil and suffering and we have to do something about it. The kingdom of God is not the church, it's one of the great heresies of history to equate the life of the church with the life of the kingdom, and only God can bring in the kingdom; we cannot build it out of building blocks, whether of doctrine or of politics: it is God's gift. But we are a signpost to the presence of the kingdom. Our life is meant to exemplify its life. The problem is that there are two ways to see the church. The first is a decaying institution, with its failures and inconsistencies; the second, the beginning of a new community, a new way of being human, which everybody is invited to experience. In this life we will always only dimly reflect the new community.

The church

I don't think there's any progressive message in the church of Jesus Christ. In every age, the wheat and the tares still grow, in every age we have our failures and our weaknesses, as well as our successes. It is God's invisible work, weaving the tapestry of human history, which we can only see dimly in our own lives, but one day we will see the whole thing, and see what God has done in our lives. I like the picture of the church which was given to us by that well-known expositor, Dr Who. He travelled through time in a battered old police box, called the Tardis. From the outside, it looked weathered and very small: you could probably just fit one person inside it. But when you went inside, you found it was bigger on the inside than it was on the outside.

The church is similar to the Tardis. From the outside it looks battered, decaying: the paint has fallen off, and statistics tell us it's very small. But walk inside the church, and you'll find it's bigger on the inside than it is on the outside. At the same time we are frustrated with the church. All of us here have things in the church which make us grind our teeth. It is essential to be frustrated with the church.

Out of the comfort zone

This sense of restlessness and frustration is essential to the Christian life, because we do not live in the world of contentment, in which we can just settle down – we are fighters. We're aware we are ordinary, human, frail, frustrated and restless, but also we know that God is at work in us, changing, loving and bringing us on as the church of Jesus Christ. In this very same church that we are frustrated with, we find the deepest love, fellowship, grace and mercy! These two things together are an essential perspective on the Christian church. We mustn't veer towards romanticism, as if we were already reigning in heaven with Christ and everything's OK; we'll just sing our songs, forget the world. Nor can we be pessimistic and despairing about the church, because God is committed to the church, Christ has died for the church! As John Stott says, 'we must not be naïve optimists or dark pessimists, but biblical realists.'

It's important that this church is a cross-cultural community; that church is not a club where we can relax with like-minded people. So many local churches have settled down with one another, implicitly giving up on mission, because they prefer the comfort of the routine of the church. How will that change the world? In Luke 6:32-36, Jesus says to us

> If you love those who love you, what credit is that to you? For even sin-
> ners love those who love them. If you do good to those who do good to
> you, what credit is that to you? Even sinners do the same. If you lend to
> those from whom you hope to receive, what credit is that to you? Even
> sinners lend to sinners, to receive as much again. But love your enemies.
> Do good and lend, expecting nothing in turn. Your reward will be great.

The love of God is not exemplified in reciprocity. If the profile of the love of God is to be seen in the life of the church, we have to love those we do not like; those we do not get on with; those who hate us. We have to cross the congregation to speak to the person we've not spoken to for years, because they have a different view of what Calvin said. We have to make friends who are not Christians, not just because we've got a mission coming up, only to drop them the week after the mission is over. How God must hate that. But we must make friends with whom we have mutual vulnerability, to whom we are committed for life, and who can see in us the life of Christ, but also the struggle.

Being real

Mission is not a public relations exercise for the kingdom of God. All too often, the church's portrayal of its own life is sweetness and light and sentiment. We have to admit to things which are deeply shaming to us; our failures, inconsistencies and injustices, because we're committed to a God of truth. We will not convince a world by hiding our vulnerabilities in the name of sentiment. We are called to be honest with one another, with the world about where we have come to in our Christian pilgrimage. The world is fed up with a church that speaks of a Christian faith which sounds too good to be true. The plans of God are good for God but often not good for us, and we go through great failure and suffering in our lives, and we've got to own it – because otherwise we cannot say we are committed to the truth.

Yet in the church, there is this wonder of unity in diversity because how are we to have a diverse congregation, unless we go with the love of God to people who are unlike us? Unless, with our hearts in our mouths, we take a risk because a risk is the obverse side of a step of faith: a risk of being rejected, laughed at, turned down. It is by taking that risk and going to people unlike us, that we cross boundaries erected by our culture, and make the church diverse. If we don't do that, it will just be a club of like-minded people. Even sinners can do that. People get on at the golf club, why shouldn't they get on in a church of like-minded people? The miracle is that people that the world thinks are enemies call each other brother and sister. That is the love of God.

Melanie Howard writes that she joined her local church in Hackney, not because she was a believer, but because she wanted her daughter to go to the church school. She is still there.

Now years into this relationship, the enduring motive for my regular pilgrimage is that church is the only place in the neighbourhood where it is possible to meet a local community of people from a wide range of backgrounds. The congregation includes Afro-Caribbeans, Nigerians, middle-class professionals, working-class families, the unemployed, single parents, older residents, and young people. The facilities are used throughout the week by a girls' youth club, a pensioners' lunch club, Brownies and Guides, women's groups, for spiritual development meetings, and as a night shelter for the homeless during the winter. It is a real centre for local activities and groups of all kinds.

Our world is turning away from individualism and isolation, longing for community, and what we need to say is, you want the community, here is the community: here is that diverse community that you long to belong to. Here is this unified group of former enemies: why is there a welcome here for you? Because of the love of God, Who accepts us as we are.

The outworking of the Christian faith is not just a thing of private virtue but entails becoming a diverse community, that city on a hill, and becoming engaged as salt and life in public life. But Christianity enters public life to fulfil its own agenda of being the signpost to the kingdom of God. The church is not interested in political life in order to promote a party or become a party or an ideology, but because it is concerned for people and their welfare. Those of us who are involved in the political life of the nation do so because of the gospel, not because we are building political empires. The Bible is concerned not just about the eternal destiny of people's souls, but the Creator God is passionately committed to justice, health and shalom for people's whole bodies and lives, now.

A divided church

One of the problems we face as the church is that as we go out to proclaim and demonstrate the great message of salvation, according to our various gifts and callings, we know that we live in a world where the church is divided. Many evangelists have said to me they go out on a limb into the world, to proclaim the gospel, and as they look back they find that somebody's sawing the branch off. They want to say, 'Look at the church!' and people look at the church and they are not encouraged by us. People may believe, but they do not want to belong. How do we approach this? The U.S. has got sixteen thousand different church groupings. Should we be embarrassed by this? Should we shrug our shoulders?

The church is not only split into the Protestant, Catholic and Orthodox wings, but into different sub-cultures. The evangelical church is split into five sub-cultures: the conservative, the contemplative, the charismatic, the radical, and the post-evangelical. These are the five sub-cultures of the contemporary evangelical movement. Each of these has its different emphases: we conservative evangelicals emphasise the message of the kingdom. The contemplative evangelical emphasises the spirituality of the kingdom. The charismatic emphasises the dynamics of the kingdom. The radical emphasises the values of the kingdom. The post-evangelical emphasises the diversity of the kingdom.

It's no sin to belong to one of these groups, no sin to draw our understanding from what being a Christian entails from its perceptions. And yet, a sign of maturity in any movement, whether it is Christian or not, is an ability to develop a self-critical perspective; an ability to laugh at oneself; to see one's own weaknesses and compromises. The evangelical movement is one which is very recent in church history, and it has as its greatest strength and its greatest weakness a borrowing from the Enlightenment tradition of the modern world. The evangelical world view is completely entwined with modernity.

One of the reasons why evangelicals are struggling is that mission will always be difficult for us until we become self-critical about the compromises we have made. One of the greatest compromises which we have been trying to rectify for the last twenty-five years has been an excessive emphasis on individualism, on salvation only for the private, personal life of the individual, and a neglect of the great swathes of Scripture that show that God is winning an entire community for Himself, and seeks to reach and reconcile the whole world to Himself.

That has got incredible consequences for those of us who are into environment and politics and economics, not just those of us who are into religion.

Generosity

I am an open evangelical. That means I have got a willingness to learn from other traditions. Recently I went through a time of darkness in my own spiritual life, and what helped me in that time was a new appreciation of the writings of Catholic writers – like Henri Nouwen, Richard Rohr and Ronald Rolheiser. They spoke to me in the darkness in a way that I was not used to being spoken to. I had to repent of my stereotyping of Catholic spirituality, and it was painful. One of the things we have to admit to is sometimes that we define the word Christian so closely that we become discouraged by God's work in the world. When I say to some of you there are 1.9 billion Christians in the world, some of you would have thought, ah but what kind of Christians are they? Could they sign the basis of faith?

We must learn to be committed to truth, to biblical revelation, but also to be open to others from other traditions who own the name of Jesus Christ and to learn from their life and not to see ourselves as self-sufficient, within the evangelical church. We conservative evangelicals have excesses – not just charismatic evangelicals! Contemplative people are sometimes spending more time with God on their knees in prayer than we in our over-activism will ever do. Those involved in radical social issues have not given up on the gospel but are trying to implement its concerns in an unjust world, and those young people who say that they are post-evangelical do not need bitter judgement and a label of traitor, but to be understood as those who are trying to receive from other traditions as well as the very fine biblical tradition of our own evangelical movement. In one word, we need generosity to one another.

I have sat through meetings in evangelical parachurch organisations, which have made me physically sick at the way in which fellow evangelicals have treated one another. The gospel is not just contained in the words of the gospel itself, but in the ways we live the gospel with each other. How can the world say, 'See how they love one another?' if we do not actually love another?

If we are to live this kind of life, we realise it's not going to be the life of super Christian, it's going to be our own, maybe inadequate offering, the life of loaves and fishes, and we must concentrate not on our inadequacy but on the adequacy of God. That is what the world wants from us – not to apply the management techniques and the ideologies of the world to Christianity so that we build effective organisations and institutions; but, in our very inadequacy, to be the people of God. In the period of darkness which I've just come through – I hope – the message which God taught me was 'trust me'. And I had to ask the question, 'Lord, what am I trusting you for in my life?' I've got my salary, my house, my insurance policies, some of us have got our health policies and our pensions sewn up, everything is sewn up. Any uncertainties, get an insurance policy, a pension plan – we do it quite sincerely in the name of Christian stewardship, but what are we trusting God for in our lives? What have we got to rely on God for?

Jim Packer's classic *Knowing God* concludes by saying that we seem to take a 'no risks' attitude to our Christian faith, as if God is not big enough for practical problems and fears. He says this

It is these half conscious fears, this dread of insecurity, rather than any deliberate refusal to face the cost of following Christ, which makes us hold back. We feel that the risks of out and out discipleship are too great for us to take. In other words, we are not persuaded of the adequacy of God to provide for the needs of those who launch out whole-heartedly onto the deep sea of unconventional living in obedience to the call of Christ. We are afraid to go all the way in accepting the authority of God because of our own secret uncertainty as to His adequacy to look after us if we do.

The future of the church is not in efficient organisation. It is not in believing we are super Christians and that the Christian life is a romantic, sentimental, wonderful life of happiness. It is in the great struggle to be faithful to God, in the great pilgrimage to get to the end, in the race to cross the line, in the mutual encouragement we need so that we may be perplexed but not in despair. It is an emphasis in a world which is anxious but has more money than it has ever had, on the adequacy of God rather than on our adequacy and our belief. And in that, if the world is going to turn to the church again and say 'see how they love one another', we have to be generous towards one another, to own the name of Christians in an increasingly hostile world. And rather than being suspicious of them, and applying our own judgements to them – by which we will one day be judged – to accept them as brothers and sisters in Christ as they do us, and encourage them as they encourage us, in our walk together in the light of God.

The Old Testament – Antiques Roadshow or Tomorrow's World?

by Chris Wright – 1998

CHRIS WRIGHT

Chris was born in Belfast, and he was ordained in the Church of England in 1977, serving a curacy in Kent. From 1983 he taught at the Union Biblical seminary, Pune, for five years as a missionary with Crosslinks, of which he is now honorary president. In 1988 he returned to the UK as Director of Studies at All Nations Christian College, and was appointed Principal there in 1993. In 2001 he left All Nations to become International Ministry Director for the Langham Partnership International, a network of ministries established by John Stott for the resourcing of the church in the developing world. He has written several books and has a particular desire to bring to life the relevance of the Old Testament to Christian mission and ethics.

The Old Testament – Antiques Roadshow or Tomorrow's World?

The *Antiques Roadshow* is a television programme which looks at a lot of old junk and decides that it's actually of considerable value, much to the surprise of those who bring the antiques along. *Tomorrow's World* is another television programme, one that looks ahead to the future and asks, 'What are the new and exciting possibilities that are there for our future world, on the basis of things that are already happening now?' So which is the Old Testament? We have to say it actually is a bit of both – it has the value of antiques and yet it also points us towards our present and indeed our future.

I want to divide this lecture up into three sections: first of all, to look at this word antique and to ask what is it about the Old Testament which gives it any value for us today. Then I'd like to think how we should go about using the Old Testament. In what ways can we understand it, particularly the Old Testament law, because for some people that is the most puzzling and difficult part? And finally we will come to that third part of the title, Tomorrow's World: what does the Old Testament have to say in terms of shaping the present and the future?

Antiques Roadshow

Old furniture may be a lot of junk, or it may have a very great deal of value. What is it that stops the Old Testament being just a load of old junk? Why should you bother to read the Old Testament? The answer is Jesus. If you go to Matthew chapters 1 to 5, you will find that Matthew wants to introduce Jesus to us. And you might have thought that, in order to introduce Jesus to us, he should begin by telling us, 'this is how He was born.' But Matthew starts a long way back and takes us through a genealogy, in the first 16 verses of Matthew, which goes from Abraham through David and right up to Jesus. It's as if Matthew is saying to us 'If you want to understand Jesus, you have to understand the story that leads to Him.' The Old Testament tells us the story that Jesus completes, the history of which Jesus is the climax. Matthew is saying to us 'Jesus didn't just suddenly appear on the earth; He actually comes as the climax of a long work of God within the people of Israel.' That reminds us that our faith is rooted in history. Why bother with the Old Testament? Because you need it if you're going to understand Jesus.

The Promise

Matthew says, five times in the first two chapters, 'This happened so what was spoken by the prophet might be fulfilled' and then he quotes a verse from Jeremiah, Isaiah, Hosea or elsewhere. He quotes not just predictions – the only one of them that was in any sense predictive is the one from Micah – but prophetic sayings in the Old Testament, which Matthew looks at in the light of Jesus and says 'Jesus fulfils the promise that the Old Testament states.' Why should we be bothered with the Old Testament? Because the Old Testament declares the promise that Jesus fulfils. All of the Old Testament is God saying 'this is what I am going to do, this is My purpose, I'm going to keep that promise and here is how I'm going to do it.' And when Jesus comes, He fulfils that promise. Without the Old Testament, Jesus doesn't make sense. The Old Testament states the promise that Jesus fulfils. He is the end of the Old Testament, not just bringing it to an end in a historical sense, but He is the end in the sense of being its destination. Jesus is the point of the Old Testament.

In Acts chapter 2, when the disciples had to explain what was happening on the day of Pentecost, Peter took them back to the Old Testament, to the prophet Joel, and said 'what you are seeing now is that which the prophet was speaking of – so you need Scripture in order to understand this.' Similarly, when Jesus was on the road to Emmaus, in order to explain to the two disciples what had happened, he took them back to the Scriptures of the Old Testament.

Identity and mission

The third thing that comes to us in those opening chapters of Matthew's gospel is the story of the baptism in the river Jordan. Jesus hears those words from His Father, 'This is My beloved Son,' or 'My Son in whom My soul delights'; translated literally, 'with Whom I am pleased.' Jesus was hearing two verses of the Old Testament Scriptures, combined together. One was Psalm 2:7, where God said about the son of David or perhaps originally about David himself, 'You are my son, this is my son, today I have begotten you.' Jesus is hearing the identity of the Davidic royal son, the king, the Messiah. The other echo is of Isaiah 42 verse 1, where God had said, 'this is My servant, in whom My soul delights, with whom I am pleased.' The servant of the Lord in Isaiah 42 and elsewhere is the one who would come, suffer and die, and represent his people, bringing God's light to the ends of the earth. The Son of God, the Davidic Messiah, the servant of the Lord, who would come and suffer, that was the identity that Jesus hears from these words from the Scriptures.

You might have thought that God could have come up with something fresh but He quoted to Jesus the Scriptures that Jesus already knew. That's my third point – it is the Old Testament Scriptures which provided Jesus with His sense of identity, Who He was, and also with His sense of mission, what He'd come to do. Time and again, Jesus went back to those Scriptures in order to be clear, to reassure Himself of what it was He had come to this earth for, and what His Father's purpose for Him was. That's why, immediately after His baptism, He went into the wilderness, and was tempted and tested, because of the vocation that He now understood He had. Each time Jesus had to take the devil back to the Scriptures. It was from the Scriptures that Jesus understood His identity and His mission; that He had come to fulfil the purposes of God. It was also from the Old Testament that He derived all His values and His teaching, as He said in the Sermon on the Mount, 'Do not think I have come to abolish the law and the prophets; I've come to fulfil them! I've come to show their continuing relevance and abiding authority over you in the kingdom of God.'

So there are three reasons, all connected with Jesus, why we should bother with the Old Testament. It tells us the story that Jesus completed, it states the promise that Jesus fulfilled, and it provided Jesus with His sense of identity and mission and values. It's antique, yes: even in Jesus' day, some parts of it were more than one thousand years old. It's priceless, because of Jesus, for Jesus, and through Jesus. I sometimes say to my students, if you want to get close to the heart of Jesus, read the Old Testament. If you want to know the heart of Jesus, read the Scriptures, because those are the stories that He knew, the songs that He sang, the promises that He read, and therefore we should read them with the same heart and mind.

The Old Testament today

What about using the Old Testament today? It's all very well to say that the Scriptures are eternal and authoritative: it's even all very well to say that all Scripture is inspired, profitable and useful for correction, training and education in righteousness and so on, but what are we to make of the Old Testament law? For many people, those laws are something of a problem. I can only offer what I hope will be a properly biblical perspective on the law, not governed by a systematic or confessional theological position. One of the problems is people come to the Bible already knowing what it says. We sometimes come to the Old Testament thinking, we already know all this law stuff, it's all fulfilled in the New Testament, it's all out of date, it's all irrelevant, Jesus fulfilled it, we don't need to bother with it, and anyway, law leads to legalism and we can't have that, we're under grace, and so it's all a bit problematic. I want us to ask the question: how does the Bible itself present the law to us? And again I want to make three points around that, of which the first is: remember that the law in the Old Testament is based upon grace. That is so fundamental that I would want to proclaim it from the rooftops.

Grace comes before Law

Let me now take you to the Scriptures. Exodus 19:4-6: the Israelites have just arrived at Mount Sinai, just as God promised they would.

Verse 3: 'then Moses went up to God and the Lord called to him from the mountain and said: "This is what you are to say to the house of Jacob and what you are to tell the people of Israel. You yourselves have seen what I did to Egypt, and how I carried you on eagles' wings and brought you to myself. Now then, if you obey Me fully and keep My covenant, then out of all the nations, you will be My treasured possession, for the whole earth is Mine, and you will be for Me a kingdom of priests and a holy nation."' Notice there what God says about Himself first. He says to Israel, 'You have seen what I have done. Before we get into the ten commandments which come in chapter 20, before we talk about the law or anything else, I want to remind you, Israelites, that three months ago, you were slaves in Egypt, being whipped and pushed around, crying out to Me in your bondage and where are you now? You are free. I've brought you out of slavery, and now you are a redeemed, liberated people. Now, let's talk about the law, let's talk about obedience and covenant.' But the words of covenant and law are given to a people who have already experienced God's redemption: nineteen chapters of redemption before you get a single chapter of law. Even the book of Exodus itself, in its shape, tells us that grace comes before law.

The point of the Law

At the end of Deuteronomy 6:20, it says 'In the future, when your son asks you, "What is the meaning of the stipulations, decrees and laws that the Lord our God has commanded us"' – the picture here is almost a family catechism going on. The father has the responsibility of teaching his children the laws of God and living by them, and at some point the son may say, 'What is all this law? Why do we keep it? What's the point of it?' The father might have simply jumped straight to verse 24: 'The Lord commanded us to obey all these decrees and fear the Lord.' Don't keep asking why, just do it, because God commanded it! All of us who are parents know the temptation to answer children's questions that way. In the case of God, that's a perfectly reasonable answer.

Why should we obey God's laws? Because he's God and he tells us to. But that's actually not the answer that the father gives. He is told by God, when his son asks him what is the meaning of the law, then he was to tell him – verse 21, 'We were slaves of Pharaoh in Egypt but the Lord brought us out of Egypt with a mighty hand and send miraculous signs, wonders, great and terrible ... He brought us out from there to bring us in and give us this land that He promised on oath to our forefathers, and that is why the Lord commanded us to keep all this law.' You see? The meaning of the law is actually to be found in the gospel, because as far as the Old Testament is concerned, the Exodus was gospel. It was God's redemption, it was God's salvation. In fact, it's the first event in the Bible that the word redemption is applied to. In the Song of Moses, in Exodus 15, after the Israelites have escaped across the Red Sea, he says, 'Lord, this is the people that You have redeemed, that You have bought for Yourself' – he's using the language of redemption, and it's there in the Exodus. And that is the reason for the keeping of the law.

That's the first point I want to make here. Obedience to the law in the Old Testament, just as much as any response we make as Christians under the New, was always meant to be a response to the grace of God. It was always to be motivated by gratitude and by feeling this is what God has done for us, and therefore how should we respond to Him? It is not the case that in the Old Testament, salvation was somehow by works and by the law. God never gave the law in order that people could be saved by the keeping of it. He gave the law to people He had saved in order that they should keep it and maintain themselves within that relationship that He had established for them so that they could continue in His blessing – all the blessings of obedience. It was the means of living out the salvation that God had given them, not the means of earning or achieving it. That was a misunderstanding that Israel later fell into, it's a misunderstanding of legalism, it's a misunderstanding which to some extent the apostle Paul was combating in the New Testament. But it is not an Old Testament perspective. The law is based on the saving grace and love of God. God acted first and said, 'Look what I've done: now, what are you to do?' It's exactly the same dynamic as you find in the

New Testament when we are told we love because He first loved us. Law is based on grace.

Mission

Secondly, the law in the Old Testament was motivated by 'mission'. You will say to me, where's mission in the Old Testament? In what sense? In the sense that in the Old Testament, God had a declared commitment to bring blessing to the nations of this world. That comes at the very beginning in Genesis chapter 12 when God called Abraham and said, 'Through you, all the nations of the earth will be blessed'. In Genesis 1 to 11, before Israel ever comes along, God is dealing with the world, He's dealing with humanity. And then because of human sin and rebellion, God called Abraham, created a people, called them into existence, and then said, 'It is through this people that I'm going to bring blessing to the nations.' That's God's mission. It's the very foundation stone of biblical mission. How does the law fit into that?

Look, for example, at two verses to try to express this particular point. In Genesis 18:19, before the law was given; you have the story of God with his two angels, on the way to bring judgement on Sodom and Gomorrah. Abraham and Sarah did not at first recognise that it was God and two angels, they simply appeared as three men at the door of Abraham's tent. They have a good meal and a conversation together and then it turns out that it actually is the Lord. The first thing He does is to renew His promise to Abraham, that he was going to have a son and that through that son, all the nations of the earth will be blessed. That is repeated in verse 18, 'Abraham will surely become a great and powerful nation, and all nations on earth will be blessed through him'. That's God's sense of purpose and mission.

Then God, with His two angels, sets off toward Sodom and Gomorrah to bring judgement on that people, and God says 'I can't keep back from Abraham what I'm going to do. I have chosen him so that he will direct his children and his household after him to keep the way of the Lord by doing righteousness and justice, so that the Lord will bring about for Abraham what He has promised Him.' So God

– and this is actually God talking to God about God – and this is pretty pure theology here, this is nothing applied, nothing systematic about this, this is just the Lord talking to Himself about Himself – and He says 'the reason that I have called Abraham is ultimately because I want to bless the nations but in order for Me to bring a link between the calling of Abraham and the blessing of the nations, this man and this people have got to live in a certain way. They've got to live according to the way of the Lord. They have got to live according to righteousness and justice' – that is the language of the law. Those are the values that you find all the way through the law and the prophets, walking in the ways of the Lord. Moses asked in Deuteronomy 10:12, 'What else does the Lord require of you, Israel, but to fear the Lord your God and to walk in all His ways?' That's what it means to obey the Lord. There is election, God's choice of Abraham, and there is His mission to bless the nations, and in between, God says, there is going to be a people committed to the ways of the Lord. The ethics of God's law is therefore the linchpin between the election of God's people and God's mission of blessing the nations.

Motivation

In Deuteronomy chapter 4:6-8, this motivation is also used by Moses as the reason for obedience that he gives to the people of Israel. In the book of Deuteronomy, Moses is constantly seeking to motivate the people to obedience, giving them reasons: because it's good for you, because it'll make you happy, because you'll be blessed, because you'll live long in the land, all sorts of reasons. In Deuteronomy 4, he tells them

> See to it that you obey and follow the laws that I have given you… Observe them carefully, for this will show your wisdom and understanding to the nations, who will hear about all these decrees and say, 'Surely this great nation is a wise and understanding people.' What other nation is so great as to have their gods near them the way the Lord our God is near us whenever we pray to Him? And what other nation is so great as to have such righteous decrees and laws as this body of laws I am setting before you today?

All of a sudden, the nations are in view. Up to this point in Deuteronomy it's been entirely God and Israel, and yet here Moses says, 'You've got to be motivated to obey God's law. If you will keep God's law as the people of God, then the nations will notice. You will be visible. Those nations around you will see a different people with a different quality of life and they will ask questions about the God you worship, and the society you have.' The motivation for keeping God's law is actually to be a witness to the nations. That is echoed elsewhere in the Old Testament. Exodus 19:6 says the same thing: 'You will be my priesthood in the midst of the nations' – the people through whom the law of God will be known to the nations. This is missionary language. We've sometimes only related it to the book of Hebrews and in relation to Jesus, but it is in 1 Peter 2, where we are also called the priesthood of God and told to live such good lives before the nations, 'that they may see your good works and then glorify God'.

So the law then is based on God's grace, that's looking back and saying, what has God done for me that I should obey Him? And it's motivated by mission – that's looking forward and saying, what is God trying to accomplish through my obedience to Him? If we could see the laws of the Old Testament in that light, it would be very helpful because it would give us a fresh perspective. This is saying: 'Here is the God Who has saved you, how should you respond? Here is the God Who wants to bless the nations, how should you respond?'

Model

The third point is this: the law was intended as a model for us to use. If God wanted to use Israel as a light to the nations, then the law was given to Israel in order to shape them into the community that actually would be a model for the nations. They were meant to be visible, to be different, to have a distinctive holiness of life that would permeate the whole of their society in such a way that when people looked at them, they would see something about God, the God of Israel. So God gave them the law as a model. They were given a constitution, a political structure, which modelled servanthood and accountability. In Deuteronomy 17, God says, 'If you want a king, you can have a king, but he is not to look like any other king you have ever seen in the world. He's not to be greater than anybody else, nor to have more wealth nor to have more women or more weapons.' If you can't have women, weapons and wealth, what is the point of being a king? But God says, 'That's the point of being a king; to be a servant, to be a pattern for the people; to be obedient to the law.' They were given political structures that modelled justice and accountability before God. They were given economic structures which would model economic equity, sharing, justice, compassion, especially for the weak and for the poor. They were given social structures of life in which the family and the household and the wider community were of great importance, in which the worth of every individual, including slaves, women, and children, was to be highly valued. Human beings, made in the image of God, were not to be treated simply according to their status and their economic value. Human needs would matter more than other people's legal rights.

This is what God wanted them to be. Now, they failed. They knew that – the prophets kept telling them. But just because they failed does not mean that the laws God gave them were therefore useless, any more than we would say in the New Testament that just because the Corinthian church had got sexual morality problems, that therefore the letter of 1 Corinthians doesn't matter. The point is, God gave them a law so they were supposed to be different. So we take that law as a model. Not as a blueprint – it wasn't given in order to say every other society on earth at every time in history and in every culture must always do exactly what Israel did, and look exactly like they looked, because obviously they couldn't and they don't! God knew that – not even in the ancient world was every society exactly the same as Israel. The law was a paradigm which provides objectives, core values, a sense of moral direction, a sense of moral priorities, which we can then use and apply when we are dealing with other societies in different cultural and historical contexts. That is the key that unlocks the Old Testament.

What kind of law is it?

We can use that key by asking questions. What kind of law is this? Is it a law which was primarily to do with Israel's social civil life, the way they would be governed; is it something which is central to their whole system, like the laws of land and family, or is it rather more marginal, on the edges? Is it a law which has to do with major covenantal and criminal offences, or is it a law simply dealing with regulating relationships between citizens or within families? Is it a law which has to do with everyday life, or is it do with religious and ritual affairs in the temple or elsewhere? And how does that affect the way we should interpret it?

Laws are different. We would not dream of interpreting all the laws in the United Kingdom on exactly the same level. You don't give quite the same weight to the bye-laws of Bournemouth city council as you do to the laws of Parliament. There is a recognition that certain laws have priorities above others. Even the Old Testament, even Jesus, recognised that. He said to the Pharisees, 'You're wonderful at keeping all the bye-laws, and you do all the little things, and you do them all very well but you have neglected the most important things in the law – righteousness, justice, mercy and love.' Even for Jesus, some things were more important that others.

Secondly, we can ask the question: what are the objectives of this particular law? What social situation does this law want to promote or prevent? If you look at any of our laws in society today, we could ask the same question. People pass laws within a community because they want to accomplish things; they want to make things better, or they want to stop abuses. We have laws in the twentieth century which seek to control abuse and to provide protection for people. So what are the objectives of the law? What group of people are going to be protected or restrained by this law? Then you look at the laws on slavery, women, debt, credit, family, land, and you ask – what is this law for? What is it trying to achieve? What are the moral principles on which it's based? As you explore those questions and begin to get some answers in an Old Testament context, you can then step back into the twentieth century and say, 'If God is the same God, and is morally consistent, then what sort of values, what sort of situations should we be concerned about now, today, in twentieth century Britain?' You move from the context of the Old Testament to the context of the twentieth century but you preserve the consistency of God and the objectives and values of His law. That seems to me to be the way we move from the one to the other. The law, then, is motivated by grace, based on grace, motivated by mission, and intended as a model and a paradigm.

Tomorrow's World

Finally, onto the third area that I wanted to bring before you this afternoon. *Tomorrow's World* was the other television programme that we looked at. Some people like to use the Old Testament to predict tomorrow's world; they've been doing that for two thousand years and consistently getting it wrong. People want to count up all the arithmetic in Daniel and work out when we're going to get raptured or they want to use Ezekiel's visions to sort out exactly when it's all going to happen in the Middle East. That's not my concern: I'm not here to use the Old Testament as some almanac to give you a timetable for the end of the world.

How does the Old Testament shape the future for us as Christian believers? Again let me give you three answers, very briefly. The Old Testament Scriptures clearly explain to us the past and the present upon which the future is based and from which it flows. There are certain fundamental worldview questions which include: where are we, what is this creation, what is this universe in which we live? The Old Testament answers with this fundamental answer: it is the world which God made, there is one God, and in the beginning He made the heavens and the earth. We also ask, who are we? What are we as human beings? The biblical answer is that we are humans made in God's image, entrusted with the stewardship of the earth and accountable to our Creator. A third question that a worldview asks is what's gone wrong, what is the reason why we're in such a mess in our world? The Old Testament answers – it is because we have rebelled against God and are disobedient to our Creator. And fourthly, the worldview question is, so what's the answer? The answer the Old Testament begins to give is that God, Who created the world, has also intervened in the world, and has begun to bring redemption, originally through the call of Abraham and the people of Israel, bringing that to its climax in the coming and resurrection of Jesus. A whole new world has begun. In the light of the Old Testament, in the light of the Scriptures, seen through the cross and resurrection and the coming of the Holy Spirit, we are given a hope, we are given security, we are given the knowledge that the God Who is our Creator is also the God who is in control. History is in His hands and the future belongs to the kingdom of God. And I hope that's a good enough tomorrow's world for us. It gives us a fairly secure place to stand.

A new humanity

The Old Testament shapes our future because it anticipates a new humanity. God called Abraham and through Abraham created Israel. And we need to see that that was God's answer to the problem of humanity. To slightly paraphrase John 3:16 – 'God so loved the world that He called Abraham and created Israel and through them sent His only Son.' God's dealings with Israel all the way through the Old Testament are always part of what God wants to do for the world of nations. The ultimate vision of the Old Testament is not just God and Israel but God and the nations. This is what you find in the worship of Israel: often, in fact, in the book of Psalms. Psalm 22:27 – 'All the ends of the earth will remember and turn to the Lord and all the families of the earth, of the nations, will bow down before Him'. That's a universal vision of a new humanity worshipping the Lord. Psalm 47 calls upon the nations to worship the God of Israel.

Look at the end of Isaiah chapter 19: it's a prophecy about Egypt and Assyria, the enemies of Israel. It's not so much talking about the historical people of Egypt and Assyria in the prophet's day – it's looking to the future, to God's great vision, and saying, 'In that day Israel will be a third along with Egypt and Assyria, a blessing on the earth, and the Lord will bless them and say, "Blessed be Egypt My people, Assyria My handwork, and Israel My inheritance".' There will be an expansion of God's people to include the nations. That note flows onwards through Isaiah: you find it again in chapter 42 where the servant is going to be a light to the nations; in chapter 49:6; you find it in Isaiah 56 where God says to the foreigner and to the eunuch – the foreigner could have no stake in the land of Israel, the eunuch could have no family in Israel for obvious reasons – and yet God says to both of them, if they choose Me, if they obey Me, if they serve Me, then I will give them a memorial better than sons and daughters, they will come to My altar, to My house of prayer, they will offer their offerings, and be accepted, because 'My house will be called a house of prayer for all nations', says the Lord.

Perhaps it was either God's sense of humour, or Luke's sense of humour, that in Acts, the very first person from outside Israel who comes within the scope of the blessing of salvation was both a foreigner and a eunuch and was reading the book of Isaiah. I'm quite sure Philip took him to chapter 56 after he'd finished chapter 53, because they didn't have chapters anyway, in those days, they just had to turn the scroll on a couple of columns, and there he was, the Ethiopian eunuch, who had come to Jerusalem to worship God but who found joy in the temple of the Lord when he found Jesus.

The Old Testament has this vision of the nations coming to be part of the people of God. And that's what led in the New Testament to the Gentile mission, when people come to faith from nations other than Israel, and it creates a huge theological problem for the church. The first theological problem the church faced was because of the success of its mission. I wish we had more theological problems like that today! How can the Gentiles be part of Israel, if they're not actually circumcised as Jews? And they had the debate: Peter spoke, Paul spoke, and then James quoted from Amos chapter 9 and says, 'Brothers, this is what the Scripture said would happen, that there would be peoples, nations, who would call on the Name of the Lord, and would be saved.' Christian mission is grounded in the Old Testament because it anticipated a new people of God.

A new creation

Finally, the third point; the Old Testament is for tomorrow's world because it anticipates a new creation. It's not just a people who are part of God's missionary vision for the future, but the whole earth, the whole cosmos. Paul says in Romans 8 that the whole of creation is straining on tiptoe, waiting for the redemption of the sons of God. Where did Paul get that idea from? The Old Testament: he was quoting Isaiah chapter 65 where God had said, 'Behold, I am creating a new heavens and a new earth and the former things will not be remembered or come to mind. Be glad and rejoice in what I will create' and that language of the creation of a new heavens and a new earth is there in the Old Testament Scriptures and it flows right through into Romans 8, into Revelation 21, into 2 Peter 2 and so on. The Bible doesn't look to us floating off to some heaven up there, pie in the sky when you die and all that. The Bible looks upon the Lord coming down from heaven to restore, to redeem, this creation. And that is a vision which is there in the Scriptures, in the Old and in the New Testament.

The Old Testament then is not just about tomorrow's world but about tomorrow's cosmos, about the whole of the universe being transformed by the living power of its Creator, redeemed, restored, and us made again in the image of Christ, as the people of God in the new Jerusalem, all the language of the Old Testament flowing together. So — *Antiques Roadshow*? Yes, in a sense, because of the priceless value that the Old Testament Scriptures have for us through the Lord Jesus Christ. And *Tomorrow's World* — yes, because it does anticipate that new people of God and that new creation of God to which we look forward with anticipation and joy.

Where Wrath and Mercy Meet

by Don Carson – 1999

DON CARSON

Professor Don Carson is research professor of the New Testament at Trinity Evangelical Divinity School in Deerfield USA. Previously he held posts at Northwest Baptist Theological Seminary, Richmond College and Central Baptist Seminary in Toronto. He has served for several years as a Pastor and has travelled in Canada and the UK teaching and preaching. He is a brilliant communicator with plenty of experience of both TV and radio and has written over forty books.

Where Wrath and Mercy Meet

Introduction: what's the problem?

Open your Bibles at Romans 3: I shall be coming to that passage in due course. For the last twenty-five years or so, I have been engaged in university missions, which have changed their shape a great deal. Nowadays, when one preaches the gospel in most universities in the western world, there is one particular area that is very hard to get across. It's not the doctrine of the Trinity: I have no trouble explaining that to university audiences, not because it is such an easy thing, but because most of them are so ignorant about the Christian faith that they don't know the tough questions! It's not the deity and the humanity of Jesus Christ – the really tough area to get across is the doctrine of sin. It's the hardest part of my job as an evangelist. This is partly because of a rising post-modern epistemology which drives many people, especially from the arts sides of the universities, to the conclusion that all notions of right and wrong are, finally, culturally dependent. They're either dependent on the individual, or the social unit, but there is no absolute right or wrong. The only absolutely wrong thing is to say that there is such a thing as a wrong thing.

This eventually has a bearing on gospel preaching, because if we cannot agree as to what the problem is, we cannot possibly agree on the solution. The result in many evangelical circles in the western world today is a kind of diluted gospel. Precisely because there is no longer any sort of universal understanding of the nature of sin, there is an increasing temptation to trim the gospel so that it is primarily given to meet your felt need. If your felt need is alienation, then Jesus is the gospel that gives you integration; if your felt need is loneliness, Jesus loves you and you will no longer feel lonely; if your marriage is on the rocks, Jesus' gospel puts together your marriage – and so on. There's a modicum of truth in all of those things, but it's only a modicum. Biblically speaking, all of those things are tied to the far more central issue. How shall men and women be reconciled to God when, by their nature and by choice, they are rebelling against their Maker and alienated from Him? If you do not have that analysis of the fundamental human problem, you cannot possibly arrive at a biblically faithful understanding of the cross.

If you begin with contemporary analyses of contemporary problems, you will always domesticate the gospel. You may begin with a contemporary analysis of a human problem, and then trace it back to a biblical analysis of the human problem, and then come to the gospel without losing the gospel. But if you don't have, somewhere or other, the biblical analysis of what is wrong with human beings, you cannot possibly remain faithful to the biblical gospel.

Back to the beginning

Let me begin by telling the Bible story in brief. In the beginning God made everything. He made human beings in His own image and likeness. He made everything good. The nature of evil is not that it is the flipside of good. It does not have the same ontological status as good, so there's a good principle and a bad principle and they sort of duke it out in the universe. In the Bible, sin is bound up with the sort of self-centredness that dethrones God.

The first question is: did God really say? And the first doctrine to be denied is judgement: you will not surely die! With the fall came an entire perversion of the created order; everything changed. In the next chapter is the first murder – fratricide. The sin becomes so appalling in the multiplying human race that God sends drastic judgement – the fall, followed by the flood. But God in His mercy does save Noah, his wife, three children and their spouses. Noah promptly gets drunk. In His mercy, God does promise never to send similar judgement again, but it is not long before the race is full of violence and evil. Some are still trying to build towers to heaven to escape floods and make themselves gods (in Genesis 11). But God humbles human arrogance there and intervenes to find one man, Abraham, and then a whole nation to come from him. Abraham is a great man, but he can be a liar. Isaac is a bit of a wimp. Jacob is the deceiver. The twelve – one of them is sleeping with his daughter-in-law; another is sleeping with his father's concubine. Ten of them are trying to figure out whether it's better to murder one of them or sell him into slavery – talk about a dysfunctional family!

Eventually they go down into Egypt, and are enslaved, and when God raises up Moses to bring them out, they have to be talked into it, quite frankly! When God does bring them out, with wonderful displays of God's control over evil, over the created order, it only takes a matter of months before the propensity of their hearts displays itself again, in the horrible incident of the golden calf. While God is graciously giving His words to Moses on the Mount, the people are in an orgy of paganism down below. Finally they enter the promised land after the first generation has died off. God gives them more miraculous signs; He preserves them through the forty years of wandering, He takes them across the Jordan river – Jericho falls, whereupon the people are already so stuffed with pride, that they make all kinds of mistakes, with respect to the Gibeonites and Ai.

Do we need to track it all out to the period of the Judges, endless cycles of rebellion and sin, followed by judgement? Eventually, there's so much judgement they cry to God for mercy, God raises up a judge, someone who leads the people in repentance yet again, delivers the people from all of their suffering. But it's only a generation or two before there's another spiral down of the cycle: horrendous paganism, the kind of paganism where you offer up your children as burnt offerings to the god of Moloch. The cycles are so appalling that by the end of the book of Judges, it's hard to read chapters 19, 20 and 21 in public. Again the refrain, 'In those days there was no king in Israel; everyone did that which was right in his own eyes.' But when the people asked for a king, they didn't ask for a king so they could be God-like and well-governed, they asked for a king so that they could be like the surrounding pagans! Saul was the result, with horrendous implications.

David, division and exile

Then God raises up a king after His own heart, David. He commits adultery and murder. One wonders what a king not after God's own heart would have done! It only takes two generations of kings before the nation splits: Israel in the north and Judah in the south. In the north, no dynasty lasts more than three or four generations, usually less than that, before it's bumped off by some new dynasty, with endless cycles of perversion and corruption, until the people are carted off into exile. And in the south, the remnant thinks that it is secure, but eventually Jerusalem falls, and in his powerful visions, Ezekiel sees the glory of God leaving the temple, and leaving the courtyard, leaving the city, parking, as it were, in a movable chariot in the mountain on the east of the city; a symbol of the judgement to come. God had abandoned His people, and they would be dispersed!

As you read through the prophets, you hear these thundering judgements from a God Who is always saying 'I am slow to anger, plenteous in mercy'. The Lord is not quickly angry; he's forebearing, and yet the threats are horrendous precisely because the sin is so appalling! This is the Bible storyline. It's how we are to understand sin. It's not because the Jews are worse than others, but because they're typical of all of us. And until we see this pattern of human rebellion against God, recycling again and again, until we see that apart from God's intervening grace, there is no enduring fidelity anywhere, we really aren't ready to see just what it is that God accomplished in Christ Jesus.

The nature of sin

Before we get to Romans 3:21, this wonderful atonement passage, we have chapter 1:18 to 3:20. The whole burden of these chapters is that God's wrath is against the entire human race, Jew and Gentile alike, because of our sin. And to get that across believably in our generation is extremely difficult. I read recently the testimony of Budziszewski in an article called *Escape from Nihilism*. Budziszewski was a moral relativist, he did his PhD to prove that all moral systems are entirely relative to their own culture, and therefore there is no absolute right or wrong anywhere. Then he eventually he was converted. He writes

> I have already noted in passing that anything goes wrong without God. This is true even of the good things He has given us, such as our minds.

One of the good things I've been given is a stronger than average mind; I don't make the observation to boast. Human beings are given diverse gifts to serve Him in diverse ways. The problem is that a strong mind that refuses the call to serve God has its own way of doing wrong. When some people flee from God they rob and kill, when others flee from God they do a lot of drugs and have a lot of sex. When I fled from God I didn't do any of those things. My way of fleeing from God was to get stupid. Though it always comes as a surprise to intellectuals, there are some forms of stupidity that one must be highly intelligent and educated to achieve. God keeps them in His arsenal to pull down mulish pride and I discovered them all. That is how I ended up doing a doctoral dissertation to prove that we make up the difference between good and evil, and we aren't responsible for what we do. I remember now that I taught those things to students – now that's sin! It was also agony. I believed things that filled me with dread. I thought I was smarter and braver than the people who didn't believe them. I thought I saw an emptiness at the heart of the universe, that was hidden from their foolish eyes. But I was the fool. How then did God bring me back?

Then he begins to explain then the nature of his conversion.

We must understand the nature of sin. Last autumn I went to spend a day in Auschwitz. I didn't see anything in the camps that I hadn't read about, and yet there was something peculiarly powerful, as many of you doubtless know, about seeing the camps for the first time. As you walk up to Auschwitz one, you see written above the gate, *Arbeit Macht Frei* – work makes you free. The place was full of vicious ironies. In one little courtyard between the buildings where tens of thousands of people were lined up against a wall and shot, you could see the place for torturing prisoners: that was the building most commonly used. And in one stone cell you could see where a figure of Christ on the cross has been etched into the stone by the fingernails of successive generations of Christians in that little chamber. You can still see the piles of human hair waiting to be shipped back from the east into Germany to make fibre; and children's clothes, glasses and shoes all ready to be recycled. You can see it all.

In Auschwitz two, most of the shacks have been burned down, the ovens have been blown up, but in Auschwitz one there wasn't time, so you can still see its gas chamber, where they could get rid of over two thousand people in about twenty minutes, using Cyclon B, a cyanide derivative. I think we in the west have often misunderstood the significance of Auschwitz. I don't want to relativise its horror. In some ways the horror was unique, in part because it was so efficient, because it combined this sort of horror with immaculate record keeping – you can still see a lot of the records. By contrast, for example, when Pol Pot was murdering, he kept no records. It was out in the jungle, and it wasn't quite as efficient. Moreover, we haven't read most of the stories of Cambodian survivors.

In this bloody twentieth century, we have not only killed six million Jews in the ovens, we have killed seven millions others; that is gypsies and other people perceived to be enemies of the German state; at least twenty million Ukrainians and others, an estimated fifty million Chinese, then the Armenian Holocaust, approximately a third of the population of Cambodia, plus the regional instances of genocide; half a million to a million – some estimate as high as a million and a quarter – Hutus and Tutsis, plus the smaller things like the Balkans. This has been the bloodiest of all human centuries so far as we can estimate. At least a hundred million people butchered, apart from the wars! And in our wisdom in the west, we have concluded that there is no such thing as evil. Now that's evil. I wish I could push this point home hard, because we are simply not ready to grasp the significance and depth and magnificence of the grace of God and the gospel until we see how deeply odious is our sin.

One of the significances, of course, of the Holocaust is that it was done by Germans. Not because Germans are the worst but because before the Holocaust, just about everybody in the western world thought of them as the best! The Germans had the best universities, the best technology, producing some of the best scholarship in the world. The nation at the technological and philosophical peak of western enlightenment values, in fact, led us into genocide. We are not better! It is of the Lord's mercies we are not consumed.

A rebel breed

If you were to read, without recreating the Bible's whole storyline, these verses from chapter 3, the average university undergraduate would think you were right over the top!

> There is no-one righteous, not even one; there is no-one who under-stands, no-one who seeks God. All have turned away, they have together become worthless; there is no-one who does good, not even one. Their throats are open graves; their tongues practise deceit. The poison of vipers is on their lips. Their mouths are full of cursing and bitterness. Their feet are swift to shed blood; ruin and misery mark their ways, the way of peace they do not know. There is no fear of God before their eyes.

I'm not for a moment denying the common grace in our hearts enables faulty, bruised, broken, rebellious sinners like you and me to do some good. But we are a rebel breed. Unless we come to terms with that sort of thing, and re-cloak it in contemporary forms so that we can get it across to people, we simply can't make the gospel clear. We simply can't.

It takes only a few hours of fast reading of the Old Testament to recognise all of this horrible sin in the Bible elicits God's wrath as its appropriate response. You just cannot read many pages of the Old Testament without coming across the wrath of God. It is always pre-sented as God's last resort, He is forbearing, but yet there are pages and pages and pages in Isaiah, Jeremiah, Amos and Ezekiel, where there is threatened judgement, and it is threatened as a function of God's wrath. The judgement that follows is not pictured in the Bible as a kind of independent result of some bad choices – you do some naughty things and there are social entailments. It is pictured, rather, as the consequence of God's wrath. But God's wrath is not portrayed as a vile temper, as an arbitrary burst of anger outside of God's control. It's pictured rather as a function of His holiness. His sheer holiness demands that those who have been made in His image, and who are but creatures, and who defy Him to His face, meet for the judgement that He Himself has already told them that they would meet. It is personal.

The cross of Christ

Now, we come to the argument in verse 21 that we Christians are justified because of the cross of Christ. The controlling expression in this paragraph is 'the righteousness of God', which occurs four times in these verses, and the word 'to justify' cognate with it, twice. I think that we shall get at the heart of the issue if we reflect on four elements.

First, in verse 21, Paul establishes the revelation of God's righteousness and its relationship to the Old Testament. 'But now,' he says, 'a righteousness from God, apart from law, has been made known to which the Law and the Prophets testify.' The 'but now' is not a logical 'now' – it is a 'now' at this point in redemptive history. In the past there has been this, but now God is doing a certain thing. That is made clear once we understand that the expression 'apart from the law' is not connected with 'righteousness of God' but 'is made known'. In other words, we are not to read 'but now a righteousness from God apart from law has been made known'. We are to read, 'but now, a righteousness from God has been made known apart from law', that is apart from the law covenant. The law covenant prescribed its own sacrificial system by which men and women could know the righteousness of God and be justified before Him, but now, at this point in the sweep of redemptive history, with the coming of Jesus Christ, the coming of the new covenant; a righteousness from God has been made known apart from the law covenant. But it is not so independent from the law covenant that it has nothing to do with it. No. It has been made known now, apart from law, yet it is that to which the law and the prophets testify (verse 21). That is to say the law and the prophets prefigured it, announced it and modelled it. But the law and the prophets did not provide it. That has happened now at the end of the age. And this righteousness is bound up with the death of Jesus Christ, with His atonement on the cross, and has been made known now at the end of the ages. That's the argument.

Judgement and grace

It is a common mistake to think that 'then there was judgement and now there's grace'. In the Old Testament, God is the God of judgement, and of grace, and in the New Testament He's still the God of judgement and of grace. I would argue that you ratchet up on both fronts. As you move from the old covenant to the new, you see the grace of God progressively disclosed in all its clarity and beauty until you see it climaxing in the cross. And if you look at the theme of judgement, yes, there's horrible judgement in the Old Testament, but it climaxes in the new with the teaching of Jesus, the apostles and Paul on hell. The only reason why we don't see the judgement likewise reaching its climax is precisely because we have relegated hell from our thinking. We do not read Revelation 14 in all its horrific imagery and say that all of the pictures of divine judgement in the Old Testament are tame compared to that. And do you know who introduces most of the innovative metaphors regarding hell in the New Testament? Jesus.

As you move from the old covenant to the new, it is not that you move from wrath to grace. You move in fact from a ratcheting up of the pictures of wrath, to wrath, and a ratcheting up of the pictures of grace, to grace! The significance rather is that now a righteousness from God has been made known apart from the law covenant. It's come in a new covenant, sealed with Jesus' blood. The old covenant did predict this. It had its lambs, its sacrificial system, its priestly system and ultimately they would find their fulfilment in the ultimate temple and the ultimate priest and the ultimate sacrifice. They bore testimony to the great sacrifice that was to come.

Faith

The second point that Paul establishes is the availability now of God's righteousness to all human beings without racial distinction but on condition of faith – verses 22 and 23. In the previous two and a half chapters, Paul has been establishing a universal guilt: both Jews and Gentiles are under condemnation. Now he says that this righteousness from God is also for all without racial distinction; Jew or Gentiles. There is a logical connection between this paragraph and the preceding chapters. 'This righteousness from God comes through faith in Jesus Christ to all who believe. There is no difference, for all have sinned and fall short of the glory of God.'

In recent years, there has been a new interpretation of the phrase rendered in the NIV 'faith in Jesus Christ'. It could be taken to mean, 'faithfulness of Jesus Christ'. The Greek could be understood that way. The word faith can mean either faith or faithfulness, it depends on the context. So it's possible to read this: 'this righteousness of God comes through the faithfulness of Jesus Christ'. After all, that is a biblical theme; the faithfulness of Jesus Christ takes Him to the cross. That's one of the great themes of John's gospel, and of the epistle to the Hebrews; He obeys even unto death. This righteousness now from God comes through the faithfulness of Jesus Christ to all who believe. Some who argue for this position say that it is clearer yet in Greek than in English, because in English, we have two different words here – faith and believe, whereas in the original it's the same root. If I were paraphrasing, it might sound a bit like this: this righteousness from God comes through faith in Jesus Christ to all who have faith. That seems a bit redundant, doesn't it? If we take it in the traditional sense, isn't that what you're forced to believe? This righteousness from God comes through faith in Jesus Christ to all who have faith; but if faith really means faithfulness, then there's no problem, they say.

I think that's profoundly mistaken. I've gradually come to the conclusion that the point of the additional phrase 'to all who believe' is precisely to establish the fact that it is not for a particular racial group as in the old covenant which was focused on the Israelites. We are to read it like this: 'this righteousness from God comes through faith in Jesus Christ to all who have faith'. In other words, you have the repetition precisely because you're stressing the 'all'. That fits the context superbly: 'this righteousness from God comes through faith in Jesus Christ to all who have faith. For there is no difference, for all have sinned and now it comes to all who have faith' – do you see? That's the point of the argument. Paul establishes this righteousness from God is available to all men and women without racial distinction but on condition of faith.

Propitiation and expiation

The third point that he establishes is the source of God's righteousness in the gracious provision of Jesus Christ is His propitiation for our sins. We are 'justified freely through the redemption that came by Christ Jesus.' Christ's death buys us back. We are justified now freely by God's grace through the redemption that came by Christ Jesus. 'God presented Him as a (older versions) propitiation in His blood received through faith.' 'God presented Him as a sacrifice of atonement' (NIV). What is at issue here? Expiation has as its object, sin. You expiate sin, you cancel sin. Expiation cancels sins. Propitiation has as its object, God. You propitiate God. You make God favourable. So the argument in the past has been: Christ's sacrifice was a propitiation, in that instead of God standing over against us in righteous wrath, His wrath was turned aside since Christ absorbed it, as it were. Christ is now favourable toward us; He's propitious toward us. He's favourable toward us, so that Christ's sacrifice is an act of propitiation which makes God favourable toward us.

Most Christians in the West believed this until the 1930s. However, in the 1930s there was a Welsh scholar by the name of C.H. Dodd. He was a brilliant scholar, known nevertheless not to be a great lover of confessional evangelicalism, and according to him, this can't be propitiation because it's so different from what propitiation means in pagan circles. In pagan circles, you propitiate the gods by your sacrifices in order to make the gods favourable. We, that are the subjects, propitiate the gods to make them favourable; the gods are the object. But that's not the way it is in Christian circles, God says. After all, God so loved the world that He gave His Son; if He was already so favourable toward us that He gave His Son, in what sense does He still need to be propitiated? He's already so propitious that He doesn't need to be propitiated! So therefore this can't be propitiation, it has to be expiation. This is not turning away the wrath of God; it's just the way God cancels sin.

Then the question becomes: why do you have two and a half chapters about the wrath of God? Start with 1:8, you see; why do you have all this stuff on the wrath of God? And he says, the wrath of God is not really wrath, it's just sort of an outworking of what goes wrong. You do naughty things and naughty things happen to you; it's a kind of moral principle in the universe. This really won't work at all; for in fact the Bible has disclosed the wrath of God throughout Scripture in both Testaments in exceedingly personal terms. If you can deperson-alise God in His wrath, why not also depersonalise Him also in His love? And then you retreat to a kind of deist perception of God; so distant and absent that He doesn't have much bearing on the present state of play. God's wrath is a function of His holiness. God is not nec-essarily wrathful. He is wrathful only as a function of His holiness: when His holiness confronts sin, He responds with judgement. But God's love is a function of His very character; God is love. He cannot be anything other than loving.

An example I sometimes use in this: picture Charles and Susan, walking down a beach, hand in hand and Charles turns to Susan and says, 'Susan, I love you, I really do.' What does he mean? He might simply mean that he wants to go to bed with her. But if we assume for a moment that he has a modicum of decency, let alone Christian virtue, then the least that he means is that he finds her utterly lovely. He is saying, 'Your eyes transfix me; you smile and you poleaxe me from about fifty yards. Your personality is wonderful, I love to be with you, it's hard for me to imagine life without you! I really do love you. I want to marry you!' He does not mean something like, 'Susan, quite frankly, your manners are grotesque. Your halitosis would frighten a herd of unwashed garlic-eating elephants. Your knobbly knees would put a camel to shame. Your personality rivals that of some mix of Genghis Khan and Attila the Hun. But I love you!' He doesn't mean that, does he?

God is love

When we proclaim our love, in part, we are proclaiming our estimate of the loveliness of the loved. But when God says 'I love you' to us, is He saying, 'You people, your smile transfixes me. I can't imagine heaven without you. Eternity without you would be just boring, I can't imagine it. Your personality is so brilliant, your education is so charming, really I love you because you're so loveable!' Is that what He means?

The fact of the matter is that God's love toward us is self-originating. He loves us because He's that kind of God, not because we're so loveable. That's why wrath and love can co-exist in God. It's hard for love and wrath to co-exist in us, because most of the time, love and wrath in us are in some measure a function of how we're reacting to externals. If I get angry with one of my kids because they haven't come in on time, some deep part of me says, 'I love you anyway; no matter what you do, I'll still love you', but on the other hand, the reason I'm upset is because they said they'd be in at such a time and they're not there!

The closest we get to seeing something of this mix of righteousness indignation, wrath and love is, perhaps, when we're rearing our kids. But sometimes we just lose it and we shouldn't: that's just wrath that is ungodly. And we don't want to get in the position of those parents who start withholding their love because the kids aren't doing what we want – 'If you don't do that, I'm just finished with you!' Isn't there a sense in which Christians will always love their kids, no matter what they do? So we can begin to glimpse what's going on in the mind of God. God stands over and against us in wrath because His holiness demands it and we are sinners, but He stands over against in love because He's that kind of God. Morally speaking, He says to us, 'You are the people of the halitosis, the horrible personality, the knees like a camel, and I love you anyway, just because I'm that kind of God.'

So in that sense, God loves us so much He gives his Son, but His wrath must still be satisfied, or God becomes an amoral being. So God presents His Son, in such a way that His Son's death removes the wrath of God. In the pagan way of things, human beings offer sacrifices and the gods are propitiated. In the Bible, God is the subject Who sends the Son, to bear our sin in His own body on the tree; to absorb the curse, to satisfy God's demands for justice; and the just dies for the unjust, and removes the wrath of God, so that God is both the subject and the object. It is in that sense that propitiation – unlike pagan propitiation – is a biblical doctrine. This notion is bound up on word study grounds with propitiation. The word that is used here is often used for the ark of the covenant, where blood was poured out on the Day of Atonement, to offer a sacrifice both for the sins of the people, and for the sins of the priest, to set aside the wrath of God before the covenant community. And here Christ shed His blood on our behalf because God presented Him, as the propitiation in His blood.

There's one more thing that I need to say about this. Sometimes we hear this illustration in Christian circles: 'It's a bit as if a judge pronounces sentence on some criminal, and then steps down off the bench, takes off their robes, and offers to take the place of the criminal.' Have you heard that sort of illustration? I'll tell you what's the matter with it.

In our justice systems, the judge is merely an administrator of justice. That's all. The judge is not personally offended by the crime. But in the case of God, the offence is against Him. There is no system of justice bigger than God. God is not an independent administrator of justice. It is His justice system, and sin, in its essence, is not merely against a system of which He is the arbitrator. It is against Him. That is precisely why He's wrathful, why He's offended. And it's precisely why – unlike our judges, who couldn't conceivably have the authority to take the place of a criminal – He can step off the bench, as it were, and provide a propitiating sacrifice that satisfies His own justice while at the same time reconciling rebellious men and women to himself.

The righteousness of God

I don't have time to cover this last one. Paul establishes the righteousness of God through the cross of Jesus Christ. God does this, we are told, to demonstrate His justice, because in His forbearance in times past under the old covenant, He had left the sins committed beforehand unpunished; they faced temporal punishments but the final handling of the sins of Abraham, or of Isaiah, or of Jeremiah, were not handled by the temple sacrifices. The final handling of those sins is what takes place in the death of Christ, so that God might be just, and the One Who justifies those who have faith in Jesus. This view of the atonement is not the only model used in the New Testament. There are other complementary models of what Christ did on the cross. But this understanding of the cross lies at the heart of all the rest of them. And if you lose this one, you lose the gospel.

I know that this point is widely disputed. Take the theme of reconciliation. Many people today say that the heart of the Pauline doctrine of the atonement is not propitiation; it's reconciliation, sinners and God being brought back together. There's no doubt that reconciliation is an important theme in Paul. The question is, why is there a need for reconciliation? The reason why we need reconciliation is because we're alienated. What has alienated us? Our sin. Why doesn't He just accept us? Because His holiness demands that He condemn us. How is it that we are reconciled to God? Christ pays for our sin, He absorbs our guilt, He takes our punishment, and you're back to wrath and substitution and propitiation as the very grounding of reconciliation. I think that you can demonstrate those sorts of points exegetically and theologically. One could treat other models of the atonement in similar ways, they all come back to this fundamental issue – what is sin? What is God's response to it? How does He deal with it? What is the purpose of the cross? And if we cannot see how ugly, how death-dealing, how God-defying sin is, we shall not see how utterly satisfying the cross is – by which alone men and women are reconciled to God.

> Long have I pondered the curse of the cross;
> sinless, the Christ bears my guilt and my pain.
> Thundering silence, a measureless cost,
> God in His heaven lets Christ cry in vain.
> Now I can glimpse sin's bleak horror and worse;
> Christ dies and bears the unbearable curse.
>
> Long have I pondered the Christ of the cross –
> gone is the boasting when I'm next to Him;
> loving the rebel, redeeming the lost,
> Jesus, pure goodness, exposed as my sin.
> Self is cast down by this triumph of grace.
> Christ's bloody cross is the hope of our race.

Contemporary Issues – World Mission

by Rose Dowsett – 2000

ROSE DOWSETT

Rose Dowsett has been a member of OMF International for over thirty years, initially spending eight years in the Philippines, working among students. Later she taught for a number of years at Glasgow Bible College (now International Christian college), lecturing in Missiology and Church history. More recently, she has been helping establish an in-service training programme for all OMF members worldwide, which takes her to many different countries. She also serves as International Chairman of Interserve International, and is a member of the Missions Commission of the World Evangelical Alliance. She recently wrote a book on mission, *Thinking clearly about World Mission*, published jointly by Monarch and OMF.

Contemporary Issues – World Mission

The Convention and Mission

Almost from its beginning and certainly by the mid 1880s, the Keswick Convention had a deep commitment to world mission. Over the years, countless people who came here met with God and found themselves compelled by His love to take the good news of Jesus Christ to every corner of the world. That world, over a hundred years ago, was a different one from ours. It was the heyday of 'high imperialism' when most of the world belonged to one of a handful of European empires. Of these, the British Empire was the biggest and most powerful. Down through the centuries, the sovereign Lord, in His great mercy, has used many human empires, sometimes to chasten His people but often to extend His kingdom.

However we may view that imperial past, a steady stream of missionaries came from the Convention. Being citizens of the British Empire, as well as of the kingdom of God, they didn't question that the world needed them. As children of their age and place, they often assumed that British culture was Christian culture, that churches anywhere in the world should look just like the one they had left behind, and that our civilisation was far superior to any to which they might go.

It has become fashionable to criticise them for their imperial arrogance and patronising attitude towards the 'natives' whom they sought to convert. But let's not forget that in an age when probably nineteen out of twenty of the world's population had never heard the gospel, when today's mass media was undreamed of and almost the only way to communicate with people was to go and talk to them, these people took seriously God's missionary mandate to the church – and went.

It cost many of them their lives. In an era when life expectancy was half of what it is today, for them it became drastically shorter still.

It took a great deal of faith and a remarkable quality of obedience to set off for China, India or Africa or the slums of British cities. They faced danger, disease, alien cultures, loneliness, privation and rejection as well as, sometimes, pure gain for the gospel's sake. Far from criticising, we should salute them and thank God that, as a result of their ministry, the church took root on every continent and in a phenomenal number of countries, people groups and tribes. It is within the past century and a half that the church has come genuinely to circle the globe, and most of that progress happened because Christian people were willing to serve God whatever the cost.

The Twentieth Century

What must it have been like, sitting in the Convention tent in 1900? The newspapers were full of the Boer war in South Africa, of skirmishes in India, of the racial hatred in the southern states of the US. During the Convention, news came in of the Boxer uprising in China, in which about two hundred missionary men, women and children and thousands of Chinese believers lost their lives. Around only 8 or 9 per cent of the world's evangelicals were then to be found outside Europe and North America, and many a place seemed one of unremitting spiritual darkness.

There followed a great outpouring of prayer and intercession but also, before the Convention finished, scores of people had dedicated themselves to take the place of those who had fallen. They poured out their prayers, their money, their futures, they offered their lives or their sons and daughters to the missionary cause. They simply didn't believe you could come to a Convention focusing on the consecrated Christian life and leave unconcerned about the unsaved of the world. God's glory was at stake, quite apart from the eternal welfare of humanity. You couldn't mean business with God and not mean business about mission. Because that was how it was at the time, for Christians, or at least Protestant believers, concentrated in Europe and North America. It went without question that the missionary movement, by definition, operated in one direction only, from the West to the rest of the world.

A mere ten years later, at the World Missionary Conference in Edinburgh, speaker after speaker confidently forecast that all the great religions of the world were hollow and would crumble fast. Within a decade or so, they said, the whole world would be Christian and civilised, so there wasn't much need to recruit more missionaries. The task would be done before most of them could reach their destination. The mood was upbeat as they focused on the gains of the past decade or so.

Today, that confidence makes us wince. It was certainly tragically misplaced. At Keswick that year, Dr F. B. Meyer said, 'If ever there was a time to send out missionaries full of the Spirit of God, it's now.' Not that the speakers at Keswick were full of gloom and doom. Jonathan Goforth, for example, reported that year on the large numbers coming to faith in China and Manchuria. But there was great realism too. The majority of the world's population still needed to hear the good news. The Keswick speakers proved to be much more accurate than the Edinburgh speakers.

Only four years later, Europe was convulsed by the first of the world wars which led to the demise of the European empires and undermined the credibility of the Christian faith in its heartlands. However, the rest of the twentieth century was by no means only one of losses. Following the Second World War, there was another huge explosion of missionary effort, particularly from Britain and North America. Administrators, evangelists, church planters, doctors, nurses, teachers, engineers, academic staff, Bible translators: all poured out in considerable numbers. Familiar long-established agencies were joined by enormous numbers of new ones, and by the last decades of the twentieth century the Western missionary force was being overtaken, numerically, by cross-cultural missionaries from Latin America, Africa and Asia.

In fact, the second half of the twentieth century presents a mixed picture. It saw the renewed confidence of Islam, Judaism, Buddhism and Hinduism and nearly half the world's population at one time were under communist regimes. In the same period many sectors of the Western churches, particularly those that had embraced liberal theology, shrank rapidly but on the other hand others held their own or even grew. In particular, the Pentecostal and charismatic churches grew in the West as well as in other parts of the world, and in Africa and Asia some indigenous churches spread like wildfire. By the century's end, the non-Western churches had far outstripped those of Europe and North America, with large percentages of sub-Saharan Africans and of Latin Americans identifying themselves as Christians.

In Asia the picture has been more complex, with some large Christian communities in a few countries, but with the overall percentage of believers in relation to total populations remaining mostly small. Over 60 per cent of the world's population is in India and eastwards, and in that area, fewer than 5 per cent would call themselves Christian. All told, the 8 or 9 per cent of a century ago of evangelical Christians in the non-Western world has mushroomed to 60 per cent.

Now I haven't taken you on this whistle-stop tour of the last century just because I'm a history addict. I believe that the Lord instructs us to be mindful of the past in order to discern how He deals with His people. But I also believe that we can't properly appreciate what is happening today unless we set it in its historical context, because the past we have inherited has largely shaped and led to our present, which will shape the legacy we leave. None of us starts from a point with no past, whether we know, acknowledge or ignore it. There is continuity as well as discontinuity in human affairs, including the affairs of the church. If we ignore this, we operate in something of an existential vacuum, or alternatively behave as though the past was still the present. Both of these tendencies are discernible in contemporary approaches to world mission. We need to understand the categories of change, and the categories of sameness both in the world, the context of mission, and in the church, the agent of mission.

Against this background, we are going now to think about our topic under four main headings. Firstly, biblical and theological issues, secondly issues of context, thirdly issues of practice and fourthly issues of attitude, and I shall be concentrating primarily on the first two. In each case I shall select one or two issues to illustrate what I think we need to explore in a far deeper way than is possible in today's lecture.

Biblical and theological issues

Probably the most sustained inspiration for the modern missionary movement has been the concluding passage from Matthew's gospel, the verses we refer to as 'the great commission'. As the last words of the Lord Jesus before His ascension, they were intended to have an electric effect on His people, and I would not wish to imply otherwise. However, being highly selective in our use of Scripture will always lead to problems, as in this case.

Firstly, there are the problems arising from the translation and understanding of these particular verses. The King James translation, which of course was once the most commonly used one, puts the emphasis on the word 'Go', but as it was originally written, the main command is 'Make disciples'. 'As you go, make disciples.' Ironically, the Authorised Version translation could reinforce the impression that only a few people were embraced within the command. After all, most were not in a position to go, if that meant overseas. We have seen how our imperial relationship to the rest of the world, and the concentration of believers in the West, made the one way traffic to 'over there' a logical conclusion. Here, it seemed, was an exclusive command for a select few. But what Matthew is saying is different. 'As you go'. Everyone goes somewhere, even if it's only to market, or into the neighbours' home. Whoever you are, as you go about your daily business, intentionally disciple those you meet. Far from being exclusive, the command is inclusive. Every Christian is to have the mind-set of a disciple maker, whether it be by encouraging other Christians to live lives more reflective of the holiness of the Lord, or by urging unbelievers to be reconciled with God and become disciples. Mission is no longer simplistically 'to go' where that means 'overseas to the heathen', but neither does it mean that there's too much to do at home, don't go anywhere else, which resonates with today's self-centred mind-set. Rather, as you go, wherever you go, in everyday local movement and also in the larger strategic undertakings to the ends of the earth, in your going make disciples. Mission is for every one of us as we go.

More important than our need to realign our understanding of these great commission verses is the need to see mission in its whole Bible context. Mission is not limited to a handful of verses, tacked on as an afterthought. It permeates the whole Bible from Genesis to Revelation, because mission is not, first and foremost, a command for us to obey: it is fundamentally a reflection of the character of God. God is by nature a missionary God, Who seeks in order to save, Who takes the initiative, Who sends first His Son and then His Spirit. The measure by which we fail to read the whole Scripture as a missionary text is the measure by which we misread it, and the measure by which God's people fail to be missionary people is the measure by which we fail to be that for which we were recreated. Our calling to mission is rooted in the character of God Himself, in Whose image we are being remade. The authentic Christian has to be a missionary Christian; the authentic church has to be a missionary church.

One of the urgent tasks facing the church today is to learn to read the whole Bible as a missionary text, with a fresh grasp of what it means to be the people of God, standing at the frontier between faith and unbelief, living out God's missionary heartbeat in the world. We have a huge hermeneutical task facing us, learning to read the Scriptures in a different way, less preoccupied with ourselves and maintaining our comfort, more concerned with how we communicate this truth to those as yet outside.

Missionary theology

Further, our biblical task is most clearly a theological task in the truest sense of the term, for if theology is wisdom and study centred on the being of God Himself, and if from Genesis to Revelation God is showing Himself to be seeking out a people to share eternity with Him, and if we are called to incarnate the kingdom of God as a powerful sign to the world, then all true theology must reflect a missionary orientation. Most Western theological textbooks revolve around far different concerns. A horrifying proportion of Western theology doesn't even revolve around God at all, let alone God as missionary. This is a critical issue for mission in today's world. Without taking account of the whole of Scripture, mission theory and practice can readily become sectional; polarising things that should stay together. And without a proper understanding of God as a missionary God, theology becomes sterile and the church wastes its energy on self-centred trivia.

The narrow biblical base on which the modern missionary movement was built has had a number of other effects, now glaringly obvious. For example, the tendency was for individuals to respond to the challenge of the great commission and then embark either on evangelism and church planting, or on medical or educational work, with the goal of seeing people converted. In neither case, however, was there a coherent doctrine of the church. How did this bit relate to that bit, indeed did it need to relate at all? Wasn't it all right to have a self-contained local congregation independent of all others, simply established along the lines preferred by the missionary? For those who came themselves from a gathered church background this all seemed attractive, the opportunity to start with a clean slate. On the other hand, for those who came from certain denominations operating on the territorial Christendom model, it seemed obvious that when you planted a new church it should come under the jurisdiction of the mother church back home, in the West, and that gradually you should bring extensive geographical areas under the one umbrella. Or what happened when you arrived in a country where there was already an existing mission work, but from a different Christian tradition from your own? The different ways of reacting to these questions caused considerable tension and sometimes some ungodly falling out.

Relational tension

Many missionaries in the early years, especially evangelicals, were focused on seeing individuals converted, but hadn't thought out what to do with them after that. In this they were simply mirroring the development of evangelicalism within the West within the matrix of Christendom. It is instructive that David Bebbington's well-known analysis of the distinctives of classic evangelicalism lists 'conversionism, the belief that lives need to be changed; activism, the expression of the gospel in effort; biblicism, a particular regard for the Bible; and what may be called crucicentrism - a stress on the sacrifice of Christ on the cross.' What is absent from these key distinctives is any focus at all on the corporate, and especially the corporate expressed in the life of the church. But now some of the unresolved questions of the past, or even the questions which were unasked, have come home to roost. Once, pioneering in another country far from home and far from other believers, questions of ecclesiology, the doctrine of the church, may have seemed too far removed from daily reality to matter, but in today's global village with rapid communication and pressing awareness of the need to relate to the world beyond our immediate community, little bits of the church here and there cannot live in hermetically sealed compartments. The issue of relationships can't be dodged.

How should different churches relate to one another, especially in the context of hostility from a dominant religion, or the government, or both? In many places, local believers imitated the example set them by the missionaries of denominational chaos, and quickly added large numbers of their own home-grown denominations. When we first went to the Philippines, we were told that there were over forty imported kinds of Baptist denomination in Manila alone, and that there were more than that again of local home-grown ones. How can you have eighty different kinds of Baptist? What are the boundaries of variation of what a church can look like in different parts of the world and still be authentically church? What should the church look like in a country where 70 per cent of the population are under twenty-one? Or where 40 per cent of the population, inside the church as well as outside, is HIV positive or has full-blown AIDS? What should the church look like in those Muslim contexts where to be an open believer is to court a speedy death? How should we relate to those professing Christian faith in the ancient churches, the Roman Catholic Church, the Orthodox Churches? Even here at Keswick we come together as a collection of individuals, with a muted doctrine of the church, with questions we do not ask. We can be, perhaps, a little too glib in saying that we are all one in Christ Jesus and any kind of structural unity or relationship is irrelevant, yet many of these questions are not only persistent, troubling and urgent in other parts of the world, they are also questions increasingly we need to address in our own country.

We need our most gifted scholars and practitioners, people passionate about mission, to think outside the familiar tram-lines of rather limited missionary thinking and much current biblical and theological enterprise, to help us face the deficiencies of the past and present and find the way ahead. I long to see an army of theologians and Bible scholars who are missionaries and missionaries who are theologians and Bible scholars, to enable the church to become more truly what she should be.

Context

Over the past thirty years or so a great deal of attention has been paid to issues of context and contextualisation. There has been much clearer recognition that, wherever we come from, we are more influenced than we recognise by our original cultures, and that this affects both our understanding of the Christian faith and how we express it. There has also been much clearer recognition of the need to remove unnecessary cultural barriers to the gospel – the principle of the Incarnation is to make truth foreign only where it has to be – and of the need to address issues in another culture that may not be part of our own. Further, we recognise that in many places there have been tremendous social changes, through industrial and technical development, urbanisation, political independence, or significant developments in education and medicine. All these and more make the world a different place from a hundred years ago. At the same time we shouldn't underestimate the innate resistance to change in many cultures. While some mass media is undoubtedly subverting some parts of some cultures, the global veneer is frequently just that, a veneer.

Let me draw attention to three particular issues of context. The first is that of the world's religions. Despite huge gains for the gospel in many parts of the world, the fact remains that particularly in recent decades, when Islam, Buddhism and Hinduism have all experienced fundamentalist revivals, the majority of those coming to faith have done so out of animism rather than out of these major religions. The Islamic, Buddhist and Hindu worlds remain largely uncracked, and these are the areas where population growth tends to be at its most explosive. You may be familiar with the 10/40 window concept, originally coined to focus on the countries and people groups living between ten and forty degrees latitude, where the Islamic, Buddhist and Hindu faiths are concentrated. The Western church and the modern missionary movement have not been well-equipped to deal with other religions.

In early years, because missionaries came from Christendom, they knew how to appeal to folk within a nominal Christian background. This was parallel with the early church evangelism amongst Jews, where the key concepts about God as personal, moral, Creator and so on were already in place, so there was a focus on the cross and the atonement, which of course is vital. But there was not so much of a focus as there needed to be on the wider picture of creation, of Incarnation, of revelation. How do we know what we know about God? It was possible to work with animists on the grounds that Western civilisation was higher, better, more evolved, so there could be a stress on education, civilisation and human evolution; sometimes, almost a kind of baptised humanism. But rather few grappled with deep questions posed by other religions. Is there any truth at all in any of them? Are they 100 per cent demonic? Are they a preparation for the gospel? Is there anything that can be approved and built on, and if so, where did that come from? How do we understand the categories, beloved by a former generation of theologians, of general revelation and particular revelation? In the West, the inability to answer these questions led to pluralism.

The critical turning point in the West, particularly here in the UK came with John Hick's call in 1985 to move from what he called Christocentrism, with Christ at the centre of your thinking and your theology, to Theocentrism. That means having God at the centre, but God became a kind of blank cheque. He said what we need is a revolution. But if you don't define God as the God and Father of our Lord Jesus Christ, you have absolutely nothing. It was a small step then to say that all religious roads lead to God, whoever, whatever God may be.

A few years ago the World Council of Churches held one of their great conferences in Canberra. It was entitled 'Come, Holy Spirit' and it began with a group of Aborigines summoning up the Aboriginal spirits. If you simply say we are talking about some spiritual reality, that is another blank cheque. What does it mean? It has to be the Holy Spirit who is part of the revealed Trinity. Here in the UK we have much greater exposure to those of other faiths today. We also have the concept of political correctness: tolerance is everything. Conviction, except about pluralism, is unacceptable. There has been a steady erosion of confidence in the uniqueness of Christ, even in some evangelical churches and a great pressure to focus on relief, development and compassion ministries, rather than evangelism and church planting. It is now easier to raise money for a new well or school than it is to support a Bible translator, church planter, or evangelist. There is an urgent, global need to study the nature of other religions, their specific content and what kind of apologetics and bridge-building are appropriate and helpful.

The second issue of context is this; we need to deal with real, specific issues in the host culture: that is, the crucial areas where conversion and change must take place for the gospel to have credibility and true engagement in that setting. It is, for example, arguable that the terrible heart-breaking slaughter of Rwanda should not have happened in a country so deeply affected by revival only a generation before. I am not questioning that that revival was a work of the Spirit of God, but the teaching and application that accompanied it focused on pietistic, limited areas of reconciliation and dealing with sin. It did not address reconciliation at ethnic level, and in many places today, even in the historically or nominal Christian world, ethnic conflict is the most terrible reality.

Take the issue of living in an environment of politically sanctioned wickedness, injustice, corruption, oppression, exploitation and poverty. In 1800 British evangelicals took on some of these things. Wilberforce, the Clapham Sect, Hannah More and Shaftesbury remain shining examples. By 1900 things weren't quite so clear, and by 1950 there was a widespread pressure amongst evangelicals to concentrate on converting people, not on political and social questions. But both the injustice and related issues were the most pressing felt needs in many places, and the gospel cannot help but be subversive in an unjust system. First in Latin America and later elsewhere, liberation theologians, mostly using a fundamentally Marxist framework, came in to fill the gaps. More recently, biblical thinkers have sought to engage with these issues, but to our shame many of them were, especially initially, accused by Western evangelicals of 'going liberal', as they were struggling with topics outside our own familiar territory. It is absurd to think that a person could live through Hiroshima, the Cultural Revolution, the Killing Fields, or the Disappeared Ones, and not ask urgent questions of God's word.

Now in many places there are important debates going on about what the kingdom looks like in this setting or that, challenging corrupt structures or deeply entrenched practices such as ancestor worship, or how you live as God's people surrounded by a million Hindu gods, or what was the fate of the generations of your ancestors who never heard of the Lord Jesus. We need to encourage our fellow Christians in this.

We in the West face unfamiliar problems. Whilst the word of God is the word of God, unchanged and unchanging, it comes with freshness and dynamic life into each new context. The gospel is not a neat but truncated four-point package, and until we reach heaven there will always be more to learn. We need our worldwide family quite as much as they need us to help us press on.

One final issue of context is post-modernism. While this most deeply impacts the West, it would be a grave mistake to think it does not already ripple far wider. The mass media see to that. You can already see the signs of it amongst the younger generation on the streets of Tokyo, Bangkok or Cairo. While few people are entirely consistently modern, post-modern or anything else, the implications for the church are staggering. Whether you are talking about evangelism or discipling or any part of the life of God's people, there are huge issues here, both for those who engage in mission and how it affects our minds, and for those amongst whom they work. We have never had so many Bibles, but we have phenomenal biblical illiteracy. We proclaim the One who is the Way, the Truth and the Life, but there have never been so many insistent culture dominating voices that tell us that there is no way, there is no truth, there is no life, only every person's licence to make the best they can of existence, however suits them best. As post-modernism is unleashed we will find ourselves, all over the world, in an environment far more hostile to the gospel than either the Jewish world into which the church was born, or the wider Greco-Roman world within which Judaism was then embedded.

Practice

First there is the issue of access and movement. Travel is easier, cheaper and speedier than it was for our friends a hundred years ago, and there are few places in the world truly inaccessible to all Christians. There are places we Brits cannot go, but maybe Brazilian or Korean Christians can. But we live in an age of visas, work permits and multiple restrictions, and Westerners in particular don't especially like dealing with unpredictable official red tape to go where they want to go. There is an enormous challenge to be creative, to find genuinely acceptable grounds for being in many places. Did you know that China has an insatiable appetite for native English speakers? Why? Because there are more mainland Chinese in formal English classes than the total population of North America. We need, prayerfully and in faith, to look for ways to reach the unreached, to think strategically about enabling those best placed, whatever their country of origin, to go to the communities where as yet there is no viable gospel witness and to declare God's saving grace in the Lord Jesus.

The second issue of practice, briefly, is responding to the sheer multi-national character of the world church and of the missionary task force. It is easy to pay lip service to this, but rather harder to follow through on the implications. In the past thirty years, God has raised up dynamic missions movements from Korea and Brazil, cross culturally within India and the Philippines and between language and ethnic groups across the continent of Africa. There are many missionary societies with marvellously multi-coloured international membership, on a scale which would have blown the minds of our friends in 1900. Yet, as I look at these same agencies, I confess that I am still troubled. On the whole, my own mission included, they still operate on western models with western approaches to decision-making, strategy, finance and structure. There is a long way yet to go if all the marvellous God-given diversity in the body of Christ is to have full expression.

But perhaps the most critical issue of all in the area of mission practice today relates to the way in which we draw on the behavioural sciences. It has been said that pragmatism is the final end of modernity, so that dominant questions are not 'what is right?' or 'what is true?', but 'what works?', 'what creates the fastest profit?', 'what gives the greatest power over the greatest number of people?' The world of mission has greatly benefited from insights and tools brought to us from the behavioural and social sciences. We have learned to look more carefully at different cultures because of the discipline of cultural anthropology. We have benefited from linguistics, we have harnessed descriptive and statistical information which may help us break down the task of mission into more manageable segments that we can get our heads around. It is good and right to grasp that the church worldwide is growing, but that this people group or that has no Scripture in their own language and no viable church. It may be helpful to apply insights from economics, or psychology, or management theory.

However, the behavioural sciences are almost all post-Christian disciplines, developed from the philosophical cradle of humanism. They are built on assumptions about the nature of human beings, and of society, which are far removed from Scripture. The most important things that can be said about human nature, that we are created in the image of God, that we are fallen and in need of being redeemed, that we have divinely ordained purpose and destination, the basis on which we are to live together, all these and more are excluded from or explicitly denied by the literature and prevailing ideas of the behavioural sciences.

I am alarmed when I see these fundamentally flawed disciplines being used uncritically as the shaping pattern for plans and strategies for the church, mission and Christian leadership. Too often we are urged to adopt methods and programmes which are born out of the assumption that we rule the universe and can put everything beneath our control, if we will but invest the resources this way or that. So we are urged to do this, that and the other thing, and then the world will be evangelised in two years, or five, or that if we would only use this strategy most people will become Christians. If there is true growth in the church, in godliness as well as number, this is the work of grace of our sovereign God, and we'd better not forget it. Yes, He invites us into real partnership with Him in the task of mission, but let's never lose sight of the fact that it is God Who creates life, Who sustains, and Who will bring all things to completion.

Yet many of these issues of practice flow from the great growth of the church and a passionate longing to see mission engaged in with all our heart and soul and mind and strength. These are great things. We give God thanks for them. Great growth inevitably spawns difficulties as well as progress: the vulnerability to heresy and the sects of large, untaught communities of young believers without Scriptures: the sense that the evangelisation of the world ought to be possible today, and many more.

Attitude

Last night we sang that inspired hymn *The Servant King*, and were reminded of Jesus' words, 'I came not to be served but to serve, and to give My life as a ransom for many', and Paul's hymn in Philippians 2, prefaced with the words 'Your attitude should be the same as that of Christ Jesus.' Here is the Lord of the Universe becoming a servant for love of a world of sinners, pouring out His life even to death on a cross. Last October I joined many church leaders, theologians, missionaries and missionary society leaders in Brazil, and the word that came over and over again from our brothers and sisters in Africa, Asia and Latin America was this

Please don't stop coming, but come and stay long enough to love us, to understand us, to be at home amongst us and in our language. Please don't come and dump your programmes and strategies on us. Please don't coerce us into doing things your way. Please come with the humility of servants and the willingness to experience alongside us persecution, suffering, weakness or even martyrdom if need be. Come and be the seed that dies. Then our people will know you really believe what you say, because you are willing to die as well as live for Jesus Christ.

We have the opportunity, maybe even the enforced inevitability of returning to the situation of the early church, where we go about our mission calling out of poverty, weakness and marginality. All around the world we need to come back not to mission done out of the power and wealth of empire, but out of humble dependence on the Spirit of God and recognition of our human frailty. Even the youngest child can grasp something of that, and of what it means to be part of God's servant army in this way.

Let me be personal. Today is my daughter's first wedding anniversary. She is celebrating it far away in Tanzania where she is working with small children. That's the fruit of a little seed planted in her heart seventeen years ago when she was a five year old gatecrasher listening in to a missionary servant here today talking to a group of young people about her work with sick and orphaned children in Africa. That day the Spirit of God planted in that little child a concern for 'little brown babies' who needed to hear and experience the love of God. Even as I speak Rachel is probably cuddling a child sick with AIDS or just frightened and in need of love.

What dreams and visions do we have for the twenty-first century? One hundred years ago our forebears' response was to commit themselves to the great cause of world mission. My prayer is that today, here in Keswick, we in our turn may have global eyes and share afresh the missionary heart of God, Father, Son and Holy Spirit. Truly we have one Lord, we are called into His one church, and we have one glorious task until He comes again.

Why I Weep for the Church
by Bishop Mike Hill – 2000

BISHOP MIKE HILL

Born in Manchester, Mike had a 'sudden conversion' to Christianity around the age of eighteen – his previous religion having been football – and from early on in his Christian life he felt God was calling him to leadership in the church. After a short business career, he trained for ordination in Cambridge, and served as both priest and rector at Chesham Bois. In 1989 he became rural Dean and in 1992 Archdeacon of Berkshire. He was consecrated Bishop of Buckinghamshire in April 1998. Mike was the UK and European chairman of the Willow Creek Association and has written two books, *Reaching the Unchurched* and *Lifelines.*

Why I Weep for the Church

I've been asked to speak about why I weep for the church. What I want to say to you, I'm saying from my heart, and actually stems from a chance comment I made when addressing a group of evangelical clergy some months ago, about my general anxiety about where we are now in our churches in Western society.

Tom Sine, in his book *Mustard Seed versus McWorld* was speaking to a bunch of aboriginal Christians. He got to the end of his talk on Genesis 3, and a large aborigine said,

'Do you mind if I make a comment?'

Tom said 'No.'

'If we abos had been in the garden in the first place, there's have been no problem!'

'Could you explain why?'

'We'd have chucked away the fruit and eaten the blooming snake!'

It would be good to think that we could rewrite bits of history, and it's not for us to rewrite Scripture. But probably we would love to rewrite parts of our personal stories: things we said that we can't take back, that we didn't mean to say; situations we would have handled differently with the benefit of that great gift, hindsight. But what about the history of the church?

In times past there were clearly things that we can rejoice about: the Reformation in Europe, the recovery of the authority of Scripture in the church, the revivalists, the nineteenth century missionary movement are parts of the church's history. But there are times when perhaps we would like to take the history book of the church and eradicate some of its pages. We think of the brutality of the crusades, the excesses of medieval monasticism, or the unchecked liberalism of sections of the Western church in the last century. Their presence stands as a blot in the church history copy book.

The church in the twentieth century

What will historians make of the church that we must take some responsibility for? The picture is, again, mixed. They will, no doubt, note that there were more Christians martyred for their faith than in any other century; though most were not members of the western church. They will chronicle the individual contributions of some great preachers and some local churches that bucked the trend. Though, in truth, there were probably less of both than we would have liked. There are too many to mention here. But the same historians will note that the century saw the church in the west in decline. Indeed, if Robin Gill from the University of Kent is to be believed, it has been in decline since the 1850s. In this country today, depending on whose statistics you believe, about 8 to 10 per cent of the population find their way into a church on a Sunday. I just stayed with my wife in Birmingham in Alabama where the equivalent figure is 65 per cent. Historian have already noted that phenomenon now known as believing without belonging. Grace Davie in her book *Religion in Great Britain since 1945* describes this well: 'believing without belonging is the description of that large gap that there is between the number of people who profess some kind of faith in God and those who actually find their way into our churches.'

I think they will add the failure of the church to mount any effective, concerted defence against secularism. Sociologist Robert Bellah has pointed out that while some of us have got excited about saving the planet – and rightly so – and expressed our faith in ecological terms, 'there seems to have been relative silence' on the destruction of something that will finish the world long before the planet gives out: namely, the destruction of our social ecology: that network of responsibilities and relationships that provide the real foundation for a civilised society. We are tempted to ask both of church and society: how did we get to where we are? I want to speak from my heart about something that is fundamental to God's plan for the salvation of the world – the church. As somebody recently said, the church is God's plan A, and there ain't no plan B.

According to Luke, when Jesus approached Jerusalem, He wept. Leon Morris in his commentary on Luke says: '"Wept" might be rendered "wailed": Jesus burst into sobbing, He lamented lost opportunity.' I want to suggest that our church historians will wish to use that phrase of the churches in the west of the last century. I, for one, weep for our church. I'm not suggesting that I can weep the tears of Jesus for His church, and my heart is certainly not as pure as His heart, and my compassion is not as intense as His compassion for the world. But let me start with two non-contentious propositions, which are these: there's nothing wrong with God and there's nothing wrong with the gospel – it is indeed the power of God unto salvation. So I conclude that there must be something wrong with our churches, and we have to be honest, to repent about that and do our utmost to rebuild God's church according to God's guidelines. As Bill Hybels said: 'Churches are an expression of Christ in the world. There's nothing like the church, there's nothing on planet earth like the wonder and the beauty and the brilliance and the power and the love and the potential of the church.' It's just that it doesn't feel like that all the time.

A declining church?

My concern for the church is not born of any negativity, disenchantment or depression. I'm as passionate about the gospel and the potential of the church as I have ever been. My willingness is born of a deep desire to see churches reach the kind of potential that Hybels spoke of. Some years ago the Christian Research Organisation produced some statistics that reflected the decline of our churches. In one of the church newspapers, the headline ran: 'Church fails to halt decline.' The following week in the same paper, the headline ran, 'Churches in decline – church leaders not worried.' A member of my church came with both copies of the paper in his hand. In some despair, he threw them on the table and said, 'Mike, what the heck will worry them?' My purpose is to address some core values that I believe we need to revisit if we are to be the church that God calls us to be. They are not issues like believers' baptism or women in ministry, or whether we should have bishops or not. Important though many of those issues are, the rest of the world does not begin to understand what the fuss is all about. I want to talk about things that are even more foundational than those, but before I move on, let me make a further couple of introductory comments.

First, Luke's gospel told us that Jesus looked at Jerusalem – the city of God, the place where the nation of Israel believed that God dwelt in a special way – and He wept. He ached because He saw that His people had not matched the privilege of their calling with the responsibility of their calling. It's not without significance that Luke tells us that Jesus went straight to the temple and attacked those who had sought to pervert one of the core functions of that temple: 'My house shall be called a house of prayer but you have made it a den of robbers'.

Where have we gone wrong? Is it fair to ask the question: 'When the nation is in rebellion, does God call His people to account?' You look at the world today and you see some good things. Most of us are better fed, better clothed, we have warmth, we have a reasonable standard of living, we're better educated, and there's a lot of good things that we can celebrate. But at the same time there's all the other stuff: the broken and damaged people, many on large doses of medication just to get them to the start line every day; the people who hide from the reality of life by abusing drugs, alcohol, or food; the moral confusion that poses as freedom; the individualism that undermines community and leaves people feeling lonely. The list could go on and on. Unless we do something to turn back the tide of self-perpetuating behaviours that ultimately bring unhappiness and destruction to communities, it will go on and on. D.L. Moody once wrote, 'I looked upon this world as a wrecked vessel. God has given me a lifeboat and said, "Moody, save all you can!"' I want to say that I believe today we need a flotilla of lifeboats.

About a month ago I turned on the television. The programme involved eight young people, all selected by being computer-matched at a dating agency. The idea was to send them to Ibiza for one week, to see if they would form a natural alliance with their computer-matched partner. When, after a night of drunken revelling, one of the girls had to ask one of the camera crew whether she had slept with one of the men because she couldn't remember, I switched over. I fear that that kind of thing is not uncommon. And I'm not telling you about it so that we can have a communal tut-tutting session. The thought that went through my mind as I watched the programme was this: what kind of church would we need to be to communicate the soul-saving, life-giving gospel to people like that? You could say that the whole thrust of my ministry has been to grapple with that one issue.

What's happened to preaching?

Here is some of my thinking on why I weep for the church. They are not tears of anger, they are not tears of boredom – well, perhaps occasionally – they are tears of frustration. The first thing is: I fear our churches are losing their confidence in preaching, even some of our evangelical churches. Anointed, biblical preaching is a necessary precursor to life change. We're told by media people that people's attention span is about twenty seconds, which appears to give the preacher limited opportunities. There are those who tell us that if we can't say it in ten minutes, then it isn't worth saying! But this is patently nonsense. Show me a great preacher whose ministry saves souls. Who would try and preach the message of salvation in ten minutes? Would Wesley or Whitfield or Edwards or Spurgeon, Dr Lloyd Jones or John Stott think that they could feed souls on such a light diet? No.

In Romans 10:14, Paul writes: 'How, then, can they call upon the one they have not believed in? And how can they believe in the one of whom they have not heard? And how can they hear without someone preaching to them? Consequently faith comes through hearing, and hearing through the word of Christ.' In Acts chapter 4, Peter and John are brought before the rulers, elders and teachers of the law in Jerusalem. The authorities are starting to get jumpy about these followers of Jesus who are growing, and worrying both the local religious establishment and the politicians. The verdict of the opponents to Christianity is clear and to the point.

In Acts 4:16-17, we read this: 'Everybody living in Jerusalem knows that they have done an outstanding miracle and we cannot deny it. But to stop this thing from spreading further among the people, we must warn these men to speak no longer in this Name.' What does this tell you? It tells you that the earliest opponents of the Christian faith were canny people. They knew that if you want to stop the church from spreading, all you do is to stop it from speaking. It's been the same ever since. Today, our opponents don't even have to issue an edict of silence because in many churches, the pastors and people have opted for a virtual silence on their own. Preaching to the converted for a few minutes inside the safety zones of our church buildings will lead to what we have – overall decline. Let's make it as least as difficult as we can for the devil.

I used the adjective 'anointed'. What does it mean? It means that the preacher's words are delivered not simply as words, but also with power, with the Holy Spirit and with deep conviction. That's the way I want to preach. It doesn't mean that if I shout at people I have God's power, or if I don't prayerfully prepare, I'm anointed. Anointed preaching asks questions of the preacher's prayer life, their study time, their holiness and their moral fibre. You can preach entertaining or erudite messages, you can make them laugh, you can make them cry, you can make them think that you're wonderful – but that's not the point. The point is changed lives. A preacher cannot run forever on an empty tank. Encourage your preachers to do less in order to prepare more, and pray more, and – in consequence – improve the likelihood of preaching that will save souls.

Biblical preaching

Our preaching must be biblical. Charles Colson wrote 'the defensive orthodoxy begins with a reverence for the authority and inerrancy of Scripture.' There is much talk about how we can make the Christian faith more accessible. But accessible doesn't mean dumbed down. My experience is that good, consistent, effective, life-changing preaching takes more theology not less, more reading not less, more preparation rather than less. And let's not forget the whole counsel of God as revealed in holy Scripture. Have we become a little selective in the themes that we preach about? Have we lost our confidence in the Bible? I have no doubt that some elements of modern psychology have helped pastors in their ministry of care. But don't forget the Bible doesn't teach that the heart of the human problem is low self esteem. It rather suggests the opposite. It actually says it's human sin – that's the diagnosis, and the prognosis is that sin that's ignored has potential eternal consequences when God exercises His final judgement. People who think that their primary problem is low self esteem don't need a Saviour. What they need, to quote Crocodile Dundee, is 'a good mate'.

How many preachers today are effectively universalists – especially at the funeral service? I'm not suggesting that preachers should get hold of bereaved people and cruelly anticipate God's judgement for them. That's unbiblical as well. But to give people false hope is also equally damaging. Finally, let me say that systematic expository preaching has its place, but, as Acts 17 shows us, when Paul preached to pre-Christian pagans, he took a different tack. He preached biblically but without obvious reference to the Bible. A preacher ought to know when to preach in expository mode, and when to preach biblically in other modes.

In our society we don't just need to preach on Christian topics. We must develop the skill of preaching Christianly on any topic. That will mean more work in the study and on our knees rather than less. As one preacher said recently, 'If revival is to come to this valley of dry bones that we are in the midst of, it will be led by preachers, not by healers, not by those who style themselves prophets in the new sense, but those who seek to convey the word of God.'

Concern for the lost?

I weep for the church because I fear our concern for the lost is not what it should be. Is there a long-standing complacency in many of our evangelical churches? At the beginning of his gospel, Luke writes he was trying to give an orderly account of the things he had experienced – to give some sense of order to it. In chapter 15, in the first few verses, is the parable of the lost sheep. The next few verses is the parable of the lost coin. The next few verses is the story that we often call the prodigal son, the parable of the lost son. Then chapter 16, the parable of a shrewd manager is a parable about a lost job and the parable of rich man and Lazarus is a parable about a lost soul. Why does Luke order his account like that? Because he's trying to put across a message that we need to re-learn in our churches: lost people matter to God.

John 3:16 says what? 'God so loved the world.' When I became a Christian, at the age of eighteen, I assumed that the gospel was great news and the church would long to share it with those who didn't know Christ. How wrong I was. The energy of the church that I joined, like many churches I know, was focused on staying in business, of maintaining an expensive building and a set of activities that left the rest of the world largely ignored. Oh, it was an evangelical church, and the minister and the curate were both enthusiastic about evangelism. But they were like John the Baptist, voices crying in the wilderness. Some years later, I was reminded of this in the church where I was minister. I was following our choir into the church one day, and it was a   family service, and the place was wall-to-wall parents and children. The last member of the choir, a man called Cyril, turned round to me, and he said to me with a sort of leer across his lips, 'I hate it in here when it's full!' Too often our churches appear more like clubs than communities. Meic Pearse and Chris Matthews in their book, *We must stop meeting like this*, wrote:

> Much of the energy of many full time leaders is taken up with preparing for and servicing the weekly schedule of meetings to fulfil the expectations of the congregation who pay their wages. And the congregation themselves are able to sleep more soundly, with consciences appeased by the thought that they have helped to employ someone who is able to see to it that the kingdom of God is advanced. What a travesty of what we are really called to be.

All of us have a significant part to play in the evangelistic task of the church and it's not happening with any consistency in many of our churches. We're not all gifted evangelists, but we are called to be witnesses who model by word and deed the values of the kingdom in our everyday lives. Sometimes being a witness means saying some of the tough things that need to be said to our society, speaking out against evil where we find it and seeking to humbly and clearly uphold God's standards for society. We must lovingly contend for the faith. Sometimes that means bearing witness within the church, and not just outside it. Let me remind you that our society in this country was built on principles and values that were shaped by the Christian faith. Today those values and principles have been badly eroded. We have to work out how best to reclaim the ground that we have lost. Why? Because if anybody knows a better foundation for the life of human communities than the word of God, then I need to know it, because I've missed something.

Dr Tim Dearborn said something that has always challenged me: 'It's not the church of God that has a mission, it is the God of mission who has a church.' What does this mean? Our English word mission comes from the Latin verb which means to send. Dearborn is saying that God is a sending God. Part of the dynamic energy of the Holy Trinity is centrifugal, it is outward. God sends His prophets. In that central act of human history, God sends His Son; His Son ascends into heaven and God sends His Spirit. There are a lot of churches in our society today which would trade under the banner of evangelical that want to put a full stop there. But God sends His church into the world. 'Go and make disciples of all the nations! You will be my witnesses to the end of the earth' – that's us. Until all God's people understand this, and more importantly, do something about it, then the church will always be a case of arrested development.

Walking the talk?

The life we've commended to others is not the life we're living ourselves.. Canadian mission theologian Dan Posterski said this: 'The world needs to see what the Christian life looks like.' One of the symptoms of the post-modern world in which we find ourselves is the very fragmented view of truth. It has been described as a pick 'n' mix approach. Post-modernists are nervous of what they call metanarratives – overarching and complete explanations of the way things are. They see such narratives as, historically, a package that their purveyors have used to hold oppressive power over people. Our calling as church is not to hold power over people but rather to live as servants in this world. Ours is not the need to oppress and force people, but rather to influence and to attract. Let me ask you a question. What do people see when they look at my life? Or your life? Lesslie Newbegin wrote that the best hermeneutic of the gospel, the best interpretation of the gospel, is a community of men and women who believe it and live it. The church, you and me, bears the big responsibility of knowing. Some people will make up their minds about God on the basis of what they see in our lives.

I have spent a lot of time in my ministry researching the attitudes of unchurched people. Many have had a bad experience of Christians which has put them off Christianity. I was in a rural parish and I found myself talking to this young woman who was an architect, specialising in church architecture. She told me about the churches that she'd worked on. I said to her, 'I'm fascinated that you're so interested in church buildings. Do you mind if I ask – are you a Christian?' That stopped the conversation dead. This is what she said, and my heart skipped a beat. Her eyes filled up and she said, 'I would love to be a Christian but the trouble is, the people I meet in your churches are such appalling people.' The trouble is that we all know a little bit of what she meant.

The extensive individualism of our times has found its way into our churches. I do wonder, given that the apostle Paul describes Christian fellowship in terms of belonging to one another, whether we retain in our churches any sense of corporate responsibility for living the life, or that when we dishonour God individually we let down the whole body of Christ locally. It's always salutary to remind ourselves that Jesus saved up his most biting criticisms for the respectable religious establishment of the day – the scribes and Pharisees and teachers of the law. Jesus called them hypocrites, people who wore a mask. It's not that making mistakes is a problem. God knows we all do that, but it's making mistakes and pretending that we don't, pretending that we're something that we're not. I teach that small group ministry is such an important ministry in today's church. My reasons for this are manifold, but it does seem to me that small groups offer the best chance we have to grow into the likeness of Christ. A small group is a place where relationships can develop to the point where we can speak the truth to each other in love. I know we're all accountable to God but my accountability to Him works best when I'm accountable to a bunch of other human beings who care about me enough to confront me with the truth about my life. We're meant to be maturing, says Paul, growing up into Him who is the head, that is, Christ. Maturity is surely an issue for many of our churches.

When Paul wrote to the church in Corinth, a church which I think rather fancied itself as a keen church, he had to tell them in 1 Corinthians 3 that he needed to feed them with milk and not solid food. In the Good News Bible the translation says, 'you still live as the people of this world live.' As far as Paul was concerned, a central characteristic of spiritual immaturity was people who still live as the people of this world live.

I don't know a better opportunity to grow that exists in our churches than the small group ministry. Until we corporately make a commitment to live the life that we are commending to others, I think we shall never have the impact that we'd like to have. 'The gospel is free,' said Dr Habgood, 'but it's never cheap.' You can't discount the teaching of Jesus without distorting it. We need to live the life we are commending to others. For instance, I think a very big deal in our Western churches is that the Bible teaches that you can't serve God and mammon. But what would a Martian make of such a claim were he to land his craft in the car park of one of our more comfortable suburban churches? We call ourselves a community but often our relationships are superficial at best and, at worst, antagonistic. Relationships have to be worked at and this brings me back to small group ministry.

One of the things that is undoubtedly compelling about the person of Jesus Christ is that He closely aligned, in His life, the message and the messenger. That's partly why His ministry challenged and transformed. If we want to build churches that challenge and transform, we have to model what we mouth. To do that is a work of the Spirit. But you've got to start, it seems to me, by wanting that to happen. Wouldn't you want it said of you, when you leave this planet, that you lived the life that you commended?

Are we strategic?

I fear that we are not strategic enough. Was Paul strategic? Did he have a plan when he set about his missionary journeys? Paul would arrive in a new town and he would immediately go to the synagogue, where people had some background of belief in God. He would open the Old Testament and seek to prove to them that Jesus was the Messiah, God's chosen one. Eventually, it appears the synagogue authorities would be a little threatened by that message, and they would throw him out, and he would go into the market place and start to preach. In Acts 17, we have a sermon that Paul preached to pre-Christian pagans. The method of preaching is clearly different. In the synagogue, Paul appealed to the Scriptures; on the Areopagus, he used a different tack – preaching biblically but without actually opening the Scriptures before them. What is your plan in your church for taking unbelieving and/or unchurched people and helping them move towards fully committed discipleship? You say, we've got a mission statement! I say, that's not enough. There's a church near us that I think has a brilliant (though I suspect not very original) mission statement. It is simply this: 'to know Christ and to make Him known'. How's that going to happen? What is their plan to help people know Christ? What is their plan to make Him known?

Too often it seems to me in our churches, we either don't have a plan or our planning is done on the basis of fantasy. We don't know enough about the people we're trying to reach but we assume that we do. Or even worse, we don't really care. When people on local church decision-making bodies start to say, 'I think what people want is…', beware! Normally what they are going to tell you is what they would like.

I think we have a need for hard data research in our churches. Some years ago I drafted a questionnaire which I sent out with some students from Cliff College, and they went around our parish, and the questionnaire had a diagnostic question, which was: would you describe yourself as a regular churchgoer? If they said yes we weren't that interested in them. If they said no, we were mighty interested. We put them through a load of questions, and one of the questions was this – this was before *Alpha* and *Emmaus* and *Christianity Explored* – if there was a small group of people who all knew nothing about the Christian faith but wanted to know more, would you be prepared to join such a group? Of those who said no, we're not regular church goers, 53 per cent said they would be prepared to attend such a group. I handed the task to my assistant minister, who was a former barrister, and who, therefore, I reckoned would be good at making the case for Christ, and we set up some small groups, and we had many, many people come to Christ in a year because of that.

If we continue to plan on the basis of fantasy, the likelihood is our plans will go nowhere slowly. A vicar from Kent recently took study leave, and for his study leave he went to work with members of his congregation. He came back and said. '95 per cent of what we do in our church is totally irrelevant.'

Spiritual gifts

The second point I want to make on the issue of strategy relates to Paul's understanding of the way the church is meant to be wired. Think of the ministry profile of many of our churches – a few people racing round like scalded cats, doing all the ministry, while the majority sit passively by and watch. And those few busy people, their health and their marriages and their relationships are coming more and more under stress. I think the church was wired with the genius of the Holy Spirit. In 1 Corinthians 12, Paul says, 'I don't want you to be ignorant about these things.' Verse 7: 'to each one the manifestation of the Spirit is given, to glorify God' and to equip the church and to serve the world. Then Paul says, 'the Spirit gives those gifts as the Spirit determines'; there is no case for claiming gifts; no place for comparisons or jealousy. The list is not an exhaustive list, but what happens if we ignore this teaching? First the church's ministry is undermined, secondly people's development is arrested, and thirdly, the church is always less than she ought to be. A theology of spiritual gifts is an excellent master plan for the church. Just imagine, for a moment, that we have the people in our churches teaching children who are gifted to teach children; if we have the people in our churches whose gift is hospitality, running the hospitality side of our churches. What if the people who are gifted in preaching preached?

The third point I want to make under this heading is that the strategy must be spiritual. Spiritual problems require spiritual strategy. We need to be praying, fasting people, who give generously; committed to learn, committed to corporate worship, who spend time in solitude. If we think we can get our strategy from the business management seminars of our land, I suspect we will miss the boat. We need to be faithful, to leave the comforts of our safety zones and to step out. The fourth point I want to make under this heading is that leadership is a vital input. Churches need to be led by those who, according to Romans 12:8, have the gift of leadership.

Let me conclude. Some of us pray for revival and I want to say to them, don't stop but don't give up on the church. Don't forget it's an important expression of God's plan for the salvation of the world. The new community of God's people is an important plan of how we are meant to bring people to Christ and nurture them to fully devoted discipleship.

But I want to end with a letter that was sent to me. It was written by a minister to the board of the Luis Palau organisation, and this is what it said:

I want you to know that sadly, on the 17th of July, my youngest daughter Rebecca, aged ten, died suddenly of a brain haemorrhage, whilst attending the funeral of her grandma, my mother-in-law, in the Isle of Man. The shock has been devastating for me and my wife and I've been off work since then, but I am resuming my duties in the New Year. My reason, though, for writing is to share that at the Southport mission on Friday the 7th of May, Rebecca responded to the invitation given by Dan Owens to give her life to Christ. At the time I shared the amusing story that as the invitation was given, and I moved forward to act as an adviser, the whole row moved with me. Rebecca and her friend were sitting at the end of the row, then me, then my son Jonathan, aged fourteen, then my wife and friend. I grabbed hold of Rebecca and told her to stay with her mother, thinking that she had misunderstood the instructions given. But she hadn't. In the days that followed, her little faith blossomed so much that I was amazed at her understanding of the things of God, at only ten and a half years old. I would find her reading her Bible alone in the garden or in her room. She wrote some very moving letters to older friends sharing her faith and copying out passages of Scripture to them. One of her favourites was Matthew chapter 6: 'Don't store up for yourselves treasure on earth, but in heaven'. In those days God was working powerfully in her life. We discovered this from other people as well. She very clearly shared her faith with her friends at school and wanted them to come to the Sunday school and church. We had a thanksgiving service in my church, soon after returning to Southport which was attended by 350 friends and people from all over the country. It was a real testimony of Rebecca's faith and has made a big impact on many people.

And this, friends, is the challenge:

> I will be very happy if you were to pass the contents of the letter onto Dan and Luis to encourage them to continue preaching the gospel and calling people to Christ at whatever age. At the Southport Theatre on that Friday night, one little girl, despite the protestations of her father, made her peace with God through Jesus Christ, Who she later wrote was 'cool'. Two months later she was dead. But we are assured she is in His care and in heaven.

I was so struck by the plea that these wonderful people made to the Luis Palau organisation; don't stop doing what God has called you to do. Preach the gospel. And don't stop doing what you do. But let all of us, as we begin a new century, pray for the vision, the imagination, the biblical integrity, the courage, the strategic intent and the faith to do it even better.

From Pulpit to Pavement
by Joel Edwards – 2001

JOEL EDWARDS

Joel is General Director of the Evangelical Alliance. Born in Jamaica, he came to Britain at the age of eight, and became a Christian soon afterwards. He was a probation officer for ten years, is a former General Secretary of the African & Caribbean Evangelical Alliance, and is a minister in the New Testament Church of God. He has written two books: *Lord Make us One* and *The Cradle, the Cross and the Empty Tomb*, both published by Hodders.

From Pulpit to Pavement

Introduction

Any notions of a lecture conjure up ideas of a definitive presentation from some expert on some subject or other. What you are about to get from me is very much a journey – a dual journey. The first comes within the context of our ministry within the Evangelical Alliance. We have been talking to about a million Christians together, developing a corporate consciousness, about being agents of change and being a movement for change for good in the nation, and that's been exercising us for the past five or six years. Some of you may have seen the literature attempting to express that in various ways. The second is a personal journey, and I guess the two things are very closely bound together. As someone who was responsible for a local church for about ten years until 1995, and is currently in public ministry, on a slightly broader platform, my own pilgrimage as an evangelical in the classical Pentecostal tradition has been one of trying to ask profound questions about the relationship between the preaching task and how that relates to the many millions of individuals who live beyond the world of the church. Those things exercise me quite significantly on a personal basis. So what I'm doing, in a sense, is allowing you the opportunity of hearing me think to myself out loud in public. They do say that it's probably the first sign of going barmy. I beg to disagree; I think you're only really in trouble if you answer yourself. As a result – and I will be sticking fairly closely to my text this morning – I hope that some of the things we raise will help you provide some of the answers along with me.

The primacy of preaching

In 1985, I began my first task as a pastor. Within about six months or so, I found myself negotiating with the architect on the fine-tuning of

the architectural designs of our new church building. We got around
to discussing where the lectern should sit. He was quite certain that it
should sit in the left-hand corner of the platform. I insisted that it
needed to stay in the centre of the platform. He was totally flabber-
gasted, totally bemused by this, he couldn't understand why anybody
should want a lectern in the middle of a church building. He
eventually gave way, but I knew that my unusual obstinacy would
actually be tea-time talk in his house. 'Guess what happened today,
dear? I met a man who…' I could hear him talking about it.

But my fixation with the centrality of the pulpit had been formed
by over thirty-five years as a classical Pentecostal. A cardinal commitment for us had always been the centrality of preaching about the
cross and about the resurrection. Preaching was and remains primary.
In fact, if you did it for less than an hour, we actually doubted your
credentials as a preacher, but don't fear, I know my time is shorter than
that!

For as long as I can remember, preaching has been sealed in my
own consciousness as a Christian. To this very day, there's no greater
sound than a voice of a man or woman telling the story in such a way
that it brings me very close to God's presence. I'm not a subscriber to
the 'we don't need sermons in a post-modern era' school of thought
at all. With all the legitimate arguments about a shorter concentration
span, and the superior impact of visual crafting, there is still a lot of
evidence that effective preaching still exists and still works. My purpose is not to consign preaching to a liturgical waste-bin. Rather, it is
a reminder of the biblical context, from which we tell the story about
Jesus and His love.

My contention is that biblical preaching is mandated to the pavement. Now preaching for the pavement is not an appeal for more
open-air services. It describes a state of mind which motivates the
preacher to preach for people rather than preaching about ideas.
When we have moved to the pavement, we don't just preach what we
have studied, we preach what people talk about. We don't just tell
people what we know, we tell them what they need to know. The
great temptation, for many of us as preachers, is that we have discovered something quite magnificent in the study. We are quite sure

that if only we had a chance to deliver this on Sunday, it would transform the world. Maybe it is what we have studied; it may not always be what people need to know.

Just like Jesus

Jesus' ministry had a very curious inauguration. When He turned up to declare His manifesto at the synagogue in Luke chapter 4, few could have imagined just how irregular He was to become. Neither His disciples, nor indeed the multitudes, would be able to find a comfortable contemporary parallel to His ministry. He was not like the scribes and Pharisees. He didn't fit in to the photo-fit of Elijah or Moses or any of the other prophets. But He did start in a very familiar place, in the synagogue. What's interesting, however, is just how short-lived His pulpit ministry was. In this respect, John's account of Jesus' work is of particular interest for us. Jesus' first pulpit appearance in John took place in Capernaum, as He explained His own peculiar relationship with God – John 6 records that for us. Thereafter, references to the synagogues are strained – chapters 9,12,16 and 18 tell of very strained relationships between the synagogue and Jesus' ministry. There may be very good reasons for this. In the first place, John, as we know, was more Hellenistic, and showed a certain amount of antipathy to the people he kept calling 'the Jews'. In any event, much of his work covers the Judean ministry rather than the ministry in Galilee. So the Temple would represent the centre of religious life as opposed to the community emphasis which we meet around the Galilean ministry in the synoptic gospels. But this doesn't actually entirely explain this migration from the pulpit to the pavement of His day. Indeed, even Matthew, the most Jewish of all the gospel writers, shares John's negative references and tensions about the religious life of the synagogue culture, and relocates Jesus' greatest sermon to a mountain slope in Galilee. We call it the Sermon on the Mount.

Something else was taking place. From the outset, Jesus was quite clear about the orientation of His preaching. Luke's manifesto made that very clear – good news to the poor, sight to the blind, freedom to the prisoner, and release to the oppressed made you look in one direction – the direction of the pavement. The sermons we remember best, including the sermon on the Mount, were preached among the people. But actually it was something far deeper than that. His manifesto marked out His audience. Jesus' focus brought a radical switch from the privileged to the poor, from the powerful to the powerless. From then on He turned out to be soft on sinners and tough on religion. Apart from the religious leaders, Jesus made no polemic statements against other people. He was always drawing them to Himself, and interestingly enough, empowering them to say 'no' to Him. Remember the rich young ruler who came to Jesus and   wanted to know how to inherit eternal life? 'You know the commandments? Do the commandments!' At the end of the encounter with Jesus, this young man couldn't quite match up. I often see, in my mind's eye, a picture of this man edging his way from the centre to the periphery of the crowd, and Jesus' eye following him. The Bible actually tells us 'Jesus looked at him and loved him'. His was the choice to reject the prophet on the pavement.

People generally got the impression that Jesus was on their side. For, curiously, He spent little time telling them how bad they were, and more time saying how much better they could actually become. Now whatever we mean by the gospel today, that is what Jesus meant by the gospel then. When He preached from the book of Isaiah that day in Capernaum, Jesus didn't change the message so much as He changed the audience. Ultimately that was probably what contributed to His death within the divine scheme of things. Jesus' example makes one thing very clear: good news primarily belongs to bad news people. If you are whole, you do not need a physician, Jesus told people. Church history holds out outstanding examples which all testify to the fact that the gospel works best when it is related to the issues of the pavement. Indeed, the vitality of the New Testament faith was due to the fact that it was integrally locked into issues which people were concerned with. New Testament doctrine grew, in part, from unsolicited revelation. God breathed into and through the apostles, as He did the prophets, in order to reveal His purposes for fallen humanity.

Mostly our faith has been shaped by the need to correct spurious ideas about Jesus which the early Christians talked about over their meals. Letters from the pulpit were attempts to deal with misguided thoughts and misguided behaviour. So from its very inception the church knew intuitively that it was meant to be a movement of the people, in the same way that Jesus taught and did (Acts 1:1). The new followers became the people of the pavement. It was Jerusalem which they filled with their gospel. Before they were clearly differentiated from the establishment, and even persecuted by them, they were already at one with the people, close enough, in fact, for their shadows and hankies to bring healing. The early Christians were typified by Dorcas and her good deeds as much as by the apostles and their teaching. You can see that in Acts chapter 9.

The pragmatism of the gospel

The history of the Christian church has been a story about the proximity of the pulpit to the people. Tertullian, a third century apologist, told the emperor of his day something which I always like to refer to, because I think it demonstrates this so well for us. 'We have filled up every place belonging to you,' he says, 'islands, your castles, your caves, your senates, your prisons, your palaces. We leave you your temples only.' The impulse to reach the people accounted for the best of the church's ministry from Assisi to Wesley and beyond. The gospel is therefore intensely pragmatic. The gospel is actually meant to work. This is precisely why miracles, revelations and unusual events tended to accompany God's proclamation amongst His people. There is a tangibility about the gospel, which we are ill-advised to divorce from the gospel.

This morning, as a time of devotion as a team, we were reading from Psalm 103 – 'Bless the Lord, my soul, all my innermost being, bless His name; bless the Lord, oh my soul, and forget not all His benefits.' It's a lecture all on its own, by the way. But if you and I took an excursion through the revelation of God among His people, right from Genesis to Revelation, we would see that God invariably encountered people through phenomena they could relate to. Nothing particularly unusual about a burning bush in the middle of a desert; something very fascinating about a burning bush which doesn't burn up, which makes me want to go see what's happening. Constantly throughout the relationship He had with His people, Old and New Testament, God consistently demonstrated Himself to be a God Who moved in the material world in such a way that people could relate His divine activity to their own subjective reality.

This is the power of the gospel and it is a fallacy, therefore, to suggest that God expects us to follow Him without any kind of payback at all. The very concept of rewards in heaven depends on the concept of God rewarding and paying back. In fact, my contention is this: so pragmatic, so practical, is the gospel, that no one is expected to follow Him if there is nothing in it for them. This is precisely the reason why revelation is invariably accompanied by manifestations of God's presence, power and provisions. Indeed, Paul made it very clear, didn't he: his own preaching, he said, came with these credentials – 1 Corinthians chapter 2: 'My preaching was not in wisdom but in demonstration of power, that your faith should not stand in the wisdom of men, but in the power of God.'

I was reading a very fascinating book by a man called Richard Fletcher, *A Conversion of Europe,* which sweeps across from the earliest days of the Christian community and right into the story of the conversion of Europe, somewhere around the third, fourth century, telling the paradigm of Christian conversion. This is how he puts it: 'Like it or not, this is what our sources tell us over and over again. Demonstrations of the power of the Christian God meant conversion. Miracles, wonders, exorcisms, temple torching, shrines smashing, were in themselves acts of evangelism.' I'm not suggesting for one moment that modern evangelicalism needs to adopt temple torching and shrine smashing as a new mode of evangelism, but I think we take the point that this compelling evidence shows people came to God when they saw something tangible, which related to their reality and turned them in the attention of the Christian God.

Proximity to the pavement was also a very powerful Reformation principle. Justification by faith went hand in hand with practical faith. Luther was obliged to wrestle with how this revolution applied to the princes as well as the ploughboy. This was precisely the thinking behind the translation of the Bible from the Latin to the various vernaculars of its day. The Protestant work ethic may be politically incorrect in the twenty-first century, but the fact is, it was essentially the impact of the gospel on working class people which instilled a hitherto unknown ethic and so elevated deprived people to a higher social status. We sometimes now call it 'redemptional lift'.

This is Alistair McGrath from a very helpful book called *Roots that refresh*: 'the Reformation', he says, 'developed sophisticated and reliable ways of allowing Christians to become deeply involved in the ways of the world while maintaining both their Christian integrity and their Christian faith.' I commend that book to you. This was not an appendix of the gospel. It is good news to the poor.

This gospel captivated evangelicalism in the eighteenth and early nineteenth century, it propelled it from the bunkers of detached individualism and made it a leading force in major reforms; ultimately, in the abolition of slavery, in people like Wilberforce, and the Clapham Sect. The historian Kathleen Eastman bore witness to this in her reflections on the evangelical witness in the first half of the nineteenth century. 'Evangelicals', she said, 'passed away from the somewhat introspective attitude of personal salvation, which it had tended to assume in the eighteenth century, to an active benevolence which attempted to demonstrate the Spirit of Christ by helping other people who were in need.' I think this commendation is very important, because it actually describes a period when evangelical commitment to social engagement was actually married to missionary enterprise and the defence of the Bible against the rising tide of secularism. It actually contributed to the birth of the Evangelical Alliance in 1846. But sadly it was not to last.

Retreat

As the nineteenth century drew to a close, there were very clear signs that the evangelical preaching was distancing itself from the pavement, and moving into retreat. The fierce challenges from the new science and the rise of secular humanism were clear reasons for this new nervousness. This was a lament taken up by R. W. Dale of the Carrs Lane Congregational church in Birmingham, in 1884; he said this: 'We are

living in a new world. The immense development of the manu-
facturing industries, the wider separation of classes in the great towns,
the spread of popular education, have urgently demanded fresh
application of the eternal ideas of the Christian faith to conduct'. And
precisely the same alarm bells were ringing from Andrew Mearns'
influential book, a book called *The Bitter Cry of the Outcast in London*,
published in 1883. Nairns warned that preaching was 'foredoomed if
it ignored the fact that social conditions could determine people's
response to the gospel'. It was a cry strong enough to influence
William Booth's work in the East End of London.

This is more than just academic history. It wasn't merely the intellectual challenge of the nineteenth century which caused the church
to lose ground to a culture hostile to the Bible. It is also its failure to
adjust to the changing demands of an industrialised society. Our withdrawal into personal piety effectively withdrew the salt from society
in the late nineteenth and early twentieth century. And this
widespread withdrawal actually made Booth's work so much more
pronounced. By the 1930s, it became evident that evangelical preaching was anxious to distance itself from a social gospel which virtually
substituted the atonement and personal salvation for good works. It
wasn't until in the 1970s, with such influences as the Messiah
Movement, Francis Schaeffer, and the growing parachurch societies,
that evangelicals redirected their gaze back to the pavement.

Preaching at the crossroads

Today's preaching is at a crossroads. In a culture more concerned with
image than content, more prone to light entertainment than moral depth,
the pulpit is definitely under threat. Preachers may no longer assume even
the right to be heard or a common language with their audience. Most
preachers grossly underestimate the growing gulf between themselves and
the culture. But we simply cannot afford to declare preaching redundant;
after all, it is still through the preaching of the gospel that God makes His
wisdom known and draws men and women to himself.

I want to suggest that that obsession with post-modernity is
unlikely to give us the best tools for effective preaching. Cultural

awareness may be the first step in the right direction, but it's not the only one. We must never diminish our need for the Holy Spirit. Was it Newton who once said: 'Prepare as though there was no Holy Spirit, and preach as though there was only the Holy Spirit'. It was a huge challenge; I'm waiting for a book to be written by someone which somehow integrates the relationship between cultural trends and spiritual trends. But I tend to see books that cover the social, political and cultural analysis to the exclusion of the profoundly spiritual analyses, and there are those who are crystal gazing on hugely speculative spiritual eschatological issues without any under-standing of the cultural and social and political trends happening in society. We need something which weaves both together and helps us to understand the place of preaching in this very, very complex and yet very, very privileged context in which God has called us to work.

But if the example of Jesus is anything to go by, we simply cannot afford to lose sight of the pavement. He it was, anointed by the Holy Spirit, who went about doing good. Jesus' driving motivation was the people, and it totally dominated His work. And He did so in two ways: firstly, by what He said, and secondly, by what He did. Acts 1:1 remains for me the abiding paradigm of Jesus' ministry. 'The former things I've written to you, Theophilus, of all that Jesus began to say and to do'. If you're a Christian, if you are a Christian worker, may be that be our guiding light. The doing of the gospel and the saying of the gospel must harmonise in our ministries.

The good preacher insists on scholarship and the proper use of the Bible. Good preaching is more than an intellectually coherent argu-ment which we all enjoy but which fails to change people's lives. Good preaching brings people closer to God. But good preaching must do more than that. Good preaching must bring us closer to our neighbours. Preaching designed for the pavement may not always have its beginning in our training or theological precision. Both are impor-tant to us if we are to keep a link between our important orthodox faith, and our Christian behaviour. If doctrine becomes weakened and relativised by our culture, it is only a matter of time before our behav-iour becomes compromised. A preacher must never neglect the Bible, but it may draw its inspiration from the lilies of the field as easily as it might the sports field. This is a constant tension for us, to balance the real world and the real world of study.

Evangelicals have been very good at preaching theology. For better or worse, our commitment to truth has been noted within the wider Christian community as well. But we've also been known for our preoccupation with the moral agenda; if we are called into public debate, it is invariably because we have been known to be against family break-down, against abortion and homosexuality, and with few exceptions we are not known to be people who are 'for' the community, 'for' people. Somehow we have managed to wrench Christ from the people and made Him a captive of our polemic arguments. Few people expect us to have anything to say about the things which really concern them: crime in our inner cities, poverty, foot and mouth disease, debt, or a positive spin on human relationships in the twenty-first century.

Prophetic preaching

Let's be quite clear: the primary task of the pulpit is to be pastoral. It is to feed the flock of God, that's what Peter was mandated to do by Jesus in John 21. That was Paul's challenge to the elders of Ephesus in Acts chapter 20. 'Feed the flock of God which He has purchased with His own blood'. And much of the Scripture is dedicated to pastoral responsibilities – Timothy, Titus and so on. But to limit the message of the church to the pastoral task is to domesticate and restrain the prophetic voice. The prophetic voice speaks outward. It will talk about sex or sanctification, it is prepared to risk being misheard, misunder-stood and mangled. Like Jesus, a prophet on the pavement is secure enough to risk being unsafe. Whilst people live their lives outside of the church building, so little preaching appears to have anything to do with such matters. That was not the New Testament paradigm at all. All of human life was embraced in the letters of the early church. Within a few words, Paul was able to move comfortably from high Christology to domestic relationships. You will see that brilliantly demonstrated in the books of Ephesians and Colossians.

Preaching should sound as though we have eavesdropped on people's private conversations. Like the Good Samaritan who went to where the injured man was, preaching for the pavement must be prepared to leave the safety of our predictable subjects, to deal with matters where people are. How will the preacher help the single people or the elderly? What message does the pulpit have to enhance marriage or parenting for our neighbours or our members? And how are people to be discipled for the world beyond the church building? And who — who — will help the politicians and the legislators develop a better idea of a community from a God's eye point of view in the twenty-first century?

Indeed, it is actually a very strange irony, this mismatch that takes place in most churches on Sundays. Don't feel too bad if this applies to you, it's just my random thoughts here. More and more leaders are in a wind-down mode, preparing for Monday's day off, preaching to people in a wind-up mode, preparing for a new week. Emotionally, it's a bit like two people passing each other in very different directions. I pastored for ten years, and then the church got smart — I had to move on, and I remember a time when our church was really going well: full attendance on Sundays, three services on a Sunday. You know, steamy windows, standing room only, and then a young woman invited me to come to her Christian Union at her university. I went along — and it was a terrifying experience.

The small band of Christians were huddled together with a slightly out of tune guitar singing hymns and choruses, almost under siege. All around them was a swirling mass of heathenism, and you could see these little huddled Christians just trying to hold on for their lives. I remember saying to Diane, the young woman who invited me along; 'Diane, is it like this all the time?' She did this: she put her hands on her hips, looked up and said, 'It's like this every day, pastor! Every day!' And suddenly I thought, 'Diane sits in front of me every Sunday. What do I give Diane to enable her to come to this place feeling fortified, ready, like a missionary, like a front-line Christian? Or am I actually giving Diane my pet subjects, am I talking to Diane, seeing her no further than the pew she sits in?' I have to confess to you that that was a salutary turning point in my ministry. You're hearing the out-workings of that all these years later because there is nothing more seductive to a preacher than a full church building.

Personal discipleship is key

An orientation to the pavement will never be satisfied with full attendance, for a packed church is absolutely no guarantee that we are making disciples of people. Every effort will be taken to ensure that every member will be – to coin a phrase – fit for life. Not merely to cope with society and the world, but to be a positive influence within it. And in an increasingly biographical culture, where personal stories have become the new bench-mark for meaning and truth and reality, personal discipleship must become the hallmark of a church fit for the twenty-first century.

Lesslie Newbiggin put it very aptly: 'The only hermeneutic or interpretation of the gospel is a community of men and women who believe it and live it.' I love that. I love the story of a young man who was telling a friend of mine about himself. They met on the underground and every so often my friend, Ozzie Williams, would see this young man preaching on the platforms and sometimes what he would do, when he got in the tube train, was to give them the gospel – a kind of moving, captive audience. One day they were on the platform together, waiting for a train, and they got into conversation. 'What do you do?' this young man asked my friend Ozzie. Ozzie said, 'I work with BT, heading for the city, that's where I work. What do you do, young man?' he asked him. 'Well,' said this young man, 'I am a Christian thinly disguised as an accountant.' And in that kind of mind-set, imagine turning loose fifty people from the local church – or five thousand people – who are disciples thinly disguised as parents and teachers and office workers and people who work in the market and people who are high-grade lecturers or high-grade business individuals zooming around and jetting around the world: Christian disciples turned loose on the world, thinly disguised as professionals, thinly disguised as workers. What a vision for a transformational church.

Philip Kenneson rather provocatively said this: 'If we could prove the proposition "God exists" is objectively true, the inhabitants of our culture would yawn and return to their pagan slumber. What our world is waiting for, and what the church seems reluctant to offer, is not more incessant talk about objective truth, but an embodied witness that clearly demonstrates why anyone should care about any of this in the first place.' In other words, we want a pulpit which touches people's lives, ministry to the pavement.

Let me tell you a story, and it's a part of my journey. For a while I was both pastoring a local church and working with the Evangelical Alliance. I remember there was a really sweltering hot afternoon mid-week and I was on the platform of Mile End Underground Station, *en route* to another church meeting with church leaders, and as I stood on the platform I was just suddenly overwhelmed with a really passionate desire not to sit with church leaders. They were very nice gentlemen but I just thought I cannot cope with being locked in a room with ten church leaders today. So I didn't go. I went to see Stanley Wellington. Stanley Wellington was dying of cancer. Stanley Wellington was the husband of Mrs Wellington, Daphne, a member of our church; a very faithful, active woman. I went along to see Stanley, sat by his bed for about two hours and chatted about absolutely nothing and everything. It was brilliant. I left Stanley's side and that would have been just a few weeks before I buried him.

Shortly after the funeral, a couple of things transpired. One was that Sister Wellington said to me, 'You know, pastor, my family see you as their pastor.' She was the only person from that family who came to church, and I know this can be replicated in many of your ministries, I'm not making a special claim to fame here. Something else more profound happened. A few weeks later one of the daughters gave herself to Jesus. What she told me, about two years afterwards, was this; 'Do you know what really drew me to the church? Do you remember the time when Dad was sick and you came along one afternoon and we were all sat on the steps outside the house, and you came along, and you sat on the steps next to us, and were just chatting with us? Then Mum came along and said, "How can you children have pastor sitting on the steps with you? Take him inside and give him a chair!" and you said to Mum, "No, it's okay, Sister Wellington, I'm very happy on the steps with the kids."' She said, that, more than anything else, made her think, my goodness, what kind of preacher is this who sits on the steps with us on a midday, midweek?

That was to be a very salutary challenge. I want to suggest to us that authentic New Testament preaching is profoundly concerned about how ministry works, and the Bible is as much concerned about our orientation in the pulpit as it is about matters of ordination in ministry. The Jesus model, the Jesus paradigm, not only said, but also did. Jesus went about doing good. This is not an appendix to the pulpit, it's a legitimate extension. Perhaps more than ever the preacher is still needed as the priest for the people, the priest for the parish, the priest on the pavement.

One more story; this one is very moving for me. About three years ago, a friend called David Shearman from Nottingham rang my office. He told Diane that he wanted to come and see me with two other friends, which is very, very suspicious. I said to Diane, 'What's the agenda?' She said, 'He didn't say; he just said he wanted to come and spend some time with you.' Along they came, all three of them, all very fatherly kind of figures from north of Watford, come to spend some time with me. Turned out that that's all they wanted to do; have fellowship! All that way to come and have fellowship! We left the office, in time for lunch, we were going around the corner for kind of a religious rite, we were going to an Indian restaurant – and on the way these three godly, fatherly men were walking with me to this restaurant. On the way we saw this young woman, and she could not have been more than in her mid-twenties, a very attractive young woman, standing on the pavement trying to dislodge something from her eye. These three men came up to this young woman and said 'You all right, love?' She said 'No'. 'You got something in your eye?' She said 'Yes.'

Quick as a flash, these three men had this young woman surrounded and I stood mesmerised next to them. One of them was holding her head, one was trying to dig a fly out of her eye with a hankie, and the other was holding her back, and she stood on the pavement, hands out, receiving. They took the fly out, they said 'there y'are, love' and they walked off, and she walked away. I will never forget that day, I am sure of it. There was this young woman with four men approaching her in broad daylight and she allows something she needs to have done to be done by these fatherly figures who have encountered her on the pavement. If they saw each other again, they would never recognise each other, but she will never forget that and it seems to me to typify the role of the church. There is a need for a church without compromise, without abandoning the message of redemption we have been entrusted with, to meet people who may from time to time be anonymous, for people who just need ministry, on the pavement.

Conclusion

When John said that the Word became flesh and lived among us, he was not thinking primarily of the cross. Even less was he thinking of those early appearances in the synagogues. The Word made flesh is only intelligible as we see Jesus, vulnerable, involved, touching and teaching the people. It was a pavement orientation. If the Incarnation means anything in the twenty-first century, it will be conveyed not only from our studious attention to the text of Scripture — often a private conversation between Christians — but it will be accomplished by the application of truth where people live, on the pavement.

Impact or Isolation – the Role of Christians in Society

by Fran Beckett – 2001

FRAN BECKETT

Fran Beckett was the Chief Executive of the Shaftesbury Society, a position she relinquished in July 2002 in order to take over the leadership of the Church Urban Fund. Converted as a teenager, she entered local authority social work and later went on to study at All Nations Christian College. She worked with UCCF in developing and supporting student witness in colleges throughout London and East Anglia. Fran is Vice-chair of the Evangelical Alliance and speaks widely on Christian social action, government social policy and leadership management. She has written several books, including *Rebuild*, a practical guide to churches on how to serve their local communities.

Impact or Isolation – the Role of Christians in Society

A different drum beat

In my office at work, opposite my desk, are two pictures by an African artist. I don't know who the artist is, but I've got these pictures because they remind me of certain things. One picture is of a group of African villagers walking along the road, talking with one another: they're quite animated, and it's just a group of people, but there's a sense of life and energy about them. I have that picture to remind and keep me focused on the importance of the good news being something for ordinary people, and that people are what God has on His heart. The second picture is of a smaller group of people, obviously African musicians, and they are drummers. They've got these beautiful long deep African drums and they're playing the drums as they walk. I have that on my wall to remind me that as Christians we should be walking, moving and living to a different drumbeat. There is something different about us, that drives and motivates us as Christians, and when we begin to lose sight of that, we're in trouble. I was very excited because the theme of Keswick, this year, is the whole theme of marching to a different drumbeat. I believe that's essential for us as Christians.

I don't know about you, but as we look at the news on the television or listen to the radio or read the papers, or just talk with people around us in our everyday lives, it's very easy to feel overwhelmed by what goes on around us, by the troubles in the world, the troubles that impact us first hand in our own lives. I guess for all of us the temptation, in the light of that, is to want to retreat back into safety behind our own front doors, or behind the walls of our churches, where things are familiar and safe. We can throw up our hands in horror at the world, and know that in our church everything will be the same.

The church can feel like a safe place for many of us. But the truth is that Jesus engages. He engaged when He came to earth, and He continues to engage with the reality of the world around us.

I want to read us some verses from John chapter 1, to remind us of the truth that our God engages with us, and engages with this world. Starting from John chapter 1, I'm going to read verses 1 and 2 and then down to verse 10:

> In the beginning was the Word, and the Word was with God, and the Word was God. He was with God in the beginning….he was in the world and though the world was made through him, the world did not recognise him. He came to that which was his own but his own did not receive him. Yet to all who received him, to those who believed in his Name, he gave the right to become children of God – children born not of natural descent, nor of human decision or a husband's will, but born of God. (Verse 14) The Word became flesh and made his dwelling among us. We have seen his glory, the glory of the One and Only, who came from the Father, full of grace and truth. John testifies concerning him. He cries out, saying, 'This is he of whom I said, he who comes after me has surpassed me, because he was before me.' From the fullness of his grace we have all received one blessing after another. For the law was given through Moses; grace and truth came through Jesus Christ. No-one has ever seen God, but God the One and Only, who is at the Father's side, has made him known.

As we think about this subject – 'Impact or isolation: the role of Christians in society', I'm going to take us through several things. First of all I'm going to look at the context, then I'm going to look at some choices, and then I'm going to look at some convictions.

Context

Twenty-first century society, the environment in which you and I live, is one of incredible change – quite fast-moving, quite unsettling for many of us, quite turbulent. It's a time of rapid and quite significant change, and not just in terms of technology. I don't know how many people here are computer whizz-kids, I'm still mastering some of it, but I can hold my own; I just don't understand the technical language. But it's not just technology that's changing, but also the realm of the assumptions that society makes about how life works. You can see that in social attitude surveys, you can see that in TV soap operas and popular programmes, you can see that in the nature of the media coverage that we have, you can see that in the thinking behind government social policy. We can see and experience it in the daily conversations that we have with people from a variety of backgrounds. There is rapid and significant change, not just in the way society works, but in the way people believe and think society should work. I want to highlight some of these things because I believe they have particular challenges and significance to us as Christians and to our role in society.

Autonomy

One of these assumptions is an increased emphasis upon the autonomy of the individual: what matters are the rights and choices of the individual. You see that in the language of stakeholders, as we read it as government policy and in our newspapers. We see it where individual experience becomes the reference point for everything. It's what I think, it's what I feel, that matters. Accompanying that emphasis upon the individual is a growing mistrust of the old ways and the old certainties, a mistrust of institutions, and authority figures. As someone who heads up a large national charity, I watch the trends of how the person in the street regards charities very carefully. From time to time surveys are issued, or the results of surveys are issued, that indicate that the general public are not just losing their confidence in charities, they're losing their confidence in government, in the police, and in the church. We see there's a decline in trust in institutions and indeed in authority figures. We see that in the disengagement of people from the political processes and the low turn-out at the last general election.

Identity

Alongside that, if there's an increased emphasis upon our autonomy and upon 'me' as a reference point, there's an incredible pressure upon people's sense of personal identity. There's a pressure to reinvent the self, if you like. I'm not sure how many of you would watch the progress of well-known rock stars like Madonna, but you will have noticed with someone like her – and she is an icon of the present age – that she has consistently reinvented herself. The drive to re-present yourself in a different package, in a different persona, in a different way; what does that say about your sense of who you are? There's a huge sense of pressure on people's personal identity.

You come across profound feelings of being alone, if you talk with people. Some of you may have come across a book that was published recently, by an American professor called Robert Putnam, called *Bowling Alone*. He highlighted a phenomenon in American society, and was arguing that Britain is entering into that phenomenon as well; where people are so cut off from one another that they even go to bowling alleys on their own. This is a communal activity, but people go on their own and they watch the television as they bowl and then they go home.

This sense of breakdown of community and isolation of one person from another is something that is growing and quite profound. There's an erosion of community and that sense of inter-dependence. This whole notion of being responsible for your neighbour becomes even more complex, when you don't know who your neighbour is. The notion of family is constantly being eroded. There's a breakdown of an understanding of committedness, of permanence in relationships. I came across a couple recently, who were celebrating their twenty-fifth wedding anniversary. They were not Christians; and they were telling me how people around them thought they were so unusual, that their marriage had lasted that long! We live in a world where we are seeing a significant erosion in the sense of permanence and committedness in relationships, in family and marriage and community.

Why am I telling you all this? We know all this. Don't we? Or do we? Our churches can act as though we live in a society that's in the 1950s rather than the early twenty-first century. If we, as Christians, are to be people who are relevant in our proclamation and our demonstration of the good news – and boy, doesn't our society need good news — we need to understand the context in which we are sharing and living that good news. Because there's a growing mistrust in the church. The church is increasingly seen as irrelevant; and those of us who claim absolute truth are seen as arrogant, presumptuous and intolerant. How are we as Christians to engage with a world that sees us like that? I have to say that that's not necessarily a view that everybody holds of all churches, and it's not necessarily a view that people, when they encounter individual Christians, feel and know of them. But nonetheless we need to read the signs of the times. Was it the men of Issachar that came to David at a time of enormous pressure in his life, and it was said of them that they understood the times and they knew what David should do? We need to be those who understand the times and therefore know what we should do.

Choices

We have a range of choices, don't we? I love the stories of King Arthur — you can imagine the castles, with their thick walls and their huge portcullises and their drawbridges. I think sometimes as Christians we're a bit like that. Imagine there's a castle; wonderful thick walls, moat around it, and across the moat, upon the hillside nearby, there's a small village. One day, with a creaking and clanking sound, the portcullis comes up and the gates swing wide open, and with a mighty crash, down comes the drawbridge and out come the Christians! They're on their white chargers, lances in hand, and they gallop across the drawbridge, over the moat, up the grassy bank to the village nearby, and they spear some poor unwary, unprepared non-Christians on the edge of their spears, turn around, gallop back across the drawbridge... Bang goes the gate, crash comes down the portcullis, up goes the drawbridge, and that's the last that's seen of them!

Surely, surely that's not the experience of the neighbourhoods around our churches? I have to say, sadly, sometimes it is. All that the community sees and knows of us is the fact that we block their driveways on a Sunday morning, or our youth group keeps them awake on a Friday night, or we call at their front door when they're

just going to find out who tried to murder Phil Grant in
Eastenders… Ding on the doorbell – it's the Christians! 'We've come
to tell you…'

Please forgive me. I have nothing against door-to-door evangelism;
I think it has its place and many people's lives have been touched and
turned around by door-to-door evangelism. But if all that our neighbourhoods and communities experience of us is that, where's the
good news for them? As we shove tracts through their doors that tell
them that they're going to hell, where's the good news for them? We
have choices. We have the choice to be those that are isolated from the
world around us, just making our occasional forays into it, in order to
rescue people from it. We have choices about whether we focus exclu-
sively on what is wrong in the world. We have choices about whether
we react to the insecurity that we feel because of such a rapidly
changing world, so that we resolve that things will never change in the
church because that's the one place where things need to remain the
same and accordingly we invest all our energies into it. Or we can
choose to recognise that we live in a context where people need to
experience the fullness of life in relationship with a God that loves
them deeply, tenderly, passionately and eternally, and to experience
that through the salvation that Christ brings. We have that choice
open to us and accordingly to live lives that demonstrate this and take
opportunity to share this with people. What will we be? What
choices will we make?

Convictions

I believe that the choices we make are informed, motivated and driv-
en by the convictions that we hold. It's our convictions that will not
only inform our choices about how to engage with a hurting world,
but also drive our decisions about our priorities and what we do. The
theme of this Convention is marching to a different drumbeat. In
other words, our convictions about the gospel, and the person of
Christ, our understanding of God's nature and His priorities, will
make all the difference to how we live our lives in the every day, when
we go home.

Identification

I want to highlight four areas of conviction that we see demonstrated
in the life of Jesus Christ. The first one is that of identification. In John
chapter 1:10; 'He was in the world, and though the world was made
through him, the world did not recognise him.' Verse 11: 'He came to
that which was his own, but his own did not receive him'; verse 14,
'The Word became flesh and made his dwelling among us.'

Some of you may have seen that version of the New Testament, *The
Message*, and in that, verse 14 is that 'God took human flesh and moved
into our neighbourhood.' Moved into our neighbourhood – God
identified with human beings! The doctrine of the Incarnation is God
with us and God for us. As we consider how we live in this world in
which God has placed us, surely the truth of God identifying with
human beings has something to say to us about the way in which we
live. As Jesus came, He confirmed the importance that our God places
upon people; affirmed the innate dignity and infinite worth of human
beings; of all human beings – not just nice ones. Not just people like
us, not just people who speak like us, who look like us, have the same
intellectual capacity as us but all human beings. The implications for
this are spelled out very clearly in John chapter 17:18 where Jesus
prays to His Father, 'As you sent me into the world, (so) I have sent
them into the world.' As Jesus was sent into the world as God Who
came amongst us and identified fully with human beings, yet without
sin, we too are sent into the world to identify with others. Not to be
like them, because the context of that verse in John 17:18 is about
holiness and sanctification; it's about being distinctive yet being sent
into the world.

I love the Authorised version where it talks about God's peculiar
people. Jesus came with a distinctiveness but with a desire to win people. If it is a conviction that we hold, as being part of the heart of the
truth of the gospel, that God identifies with human beings, then the
option of retreating into our churches is not open to us. If that is truly
a conviction we hold, then we are called to roll up our sleeves and
identify as Jesus did; to be fully engaged, yet distinctive; to be in the
world but not of the world. Yes, society may be disillusioned about

institutions, it may see the church as irrelevant; but people are crying out for relationship. Have you noticed the trend on the television of the growing number of programmes, many of them American, all about friendship – and the continuing popularity of the Channel 4 progamme *Friends*? There has been series after series of that and similar programmes, where people are looking for friendship, they're looking for relationship: they may be disillusioned with institutions but they're still looking for relationship.

Identifying, getting alongside, being there for people – I think that poses some questions for us in our churches about what our priorities are. Do we, in our churches, demand attendance after attendance after attendance at meeting after meeting after meeting, and your spirituality and your level of spiritual maturity is judged by the number of meetings you manage to attend? And at the same time you're expected, if you're married, to be a good wife or a good husband, and a good parent, and if you're working, you're supposed to be faithful in the workplace and by the way, you're supposed to be a good neighbour, and by the way you're supposed to be at every meeting in the church? Is it do-able? Is it? Do you wonder why we see a decline in the numbers of younger people attending churches, younger people who are very committed as Christians? They cannot do it all! In our churches we need to have structures, and teaching, and means to equip people for engaging with the world around, where they are taught and discipled, and supported and prayed for and sent out to engage with the world.

My church is going through a very interesting time. We don't have our own building, and the building we did have was taken away from us at Christmas – the owners decided they wanted to do something else with it. We haven't had a church building now for months. We do have somewhere to meet but it's mid-week, so Sunday morning church cannot be held in the same way. It has been extremely insecure-making! Some people have found it incredibly difficult. For others, it's been the making of them. People have found a new vibrancy in their faith, a new committtedness to share Jesus where they are in their day-to-day lives. We hold church in the open air, whenever we can, depending on the weather – and even not depending on the weather! – on a Sunday morning, and it's not an open air where we're preaching at the crowds; we're just being church together. And the numbers of people that come and join us and come and stand and come and talk to us!   The sense of pressure isn't there upon us to go out and witness. It happens very naturally. There's something about having moved away, from all that is just the structure of keeping it going, to the reality of the heart of it all. What are the priorities in our local churches? Is it to keep it the same as it's ever been? Or is to equip – to motivate – to support – and to enable us to be Christians where God has placed us in the day-to-day?

God's passion for people

I unashamedly will speak about that any opportunity I get; in fact, any subject I am given, somehow that will come into it – because I believe with a certainty, and I believe that the word of God teaches us, and my experience tells me, that our God is passionate about people! This is no weak, sentimental, Mills and Boon, Barbara Cartland fluffy pink God that we worship and we serve. This is the God of the whole universe; the God that created this universe, Who holds it in place, Who created human beings at the very pinnacle of His creation and looked on us and said: 'These are very good!' Very good! He demonstrated His passion for His people by sending His only Son to come and to die for us. Oh, how we need to grasp and to be gripped by the truth and the reality that God is passionate about people! Because as we are gripped by that personally, and we experience it personally, that will just spill over from our lives, wherever we go. As a fairly pagan teenager, John 3:16 was probably the first verse I was taught. 'For God so loved the world' – that means people like you and me; people like our neighbour; people like the woman on the supermarket checkout, people whom I'm sometimes with on the London Underground.

What sort of world do we live in? Isn't this a world that needs to know good news? Our God is passionate about people, not a pink fluffy sentimental sort of feeling, but a love for us that knows everything there is to know about us and loves us just the same! He laid down His life for us. Compare that with our busy, and preoccupied lives. This is a story I tell quite a lot. Thomas Jefferson, the American president, is out travelling on horseback with his men. It's been a time of torrential rain, and they come to a river that is in full flood. They get off their horses, and start, very carefully, to lead the horses across this river. It's very treacherous, difficult to get a foothold. There's a stranger on the bank, watching them. He comes up to them when they've got to the other side and he walks straight through the group, to Thomas Jefferson, the president. You must hear the intake of breath as he does that. He says, 'Sir, will you help me across the river?' Without a further word, the president gets down off his horse and helps him back across the river. Later, when this man was asked, 'Don't you realise who it was you approached? The president of the United States!', he replied: 'All I know is across your faces was written the word "no" and on his word was written the word "yes".' What do we have written across our faces as we engage with people around us, as we travel to and from work, as we go to the shops, as we meet our neighbours, in our families, down at the post office, in the library, wherever it is we go? Do we have the word 'yes' written across our faces, or do we have 'no' faces? Do you know what I mean by a 'no' face? 'Don't bother me, I'm too busy! I'm in a hurry, I've got things on my mind!' You know the rubber-neck syndrome in churches? It's when you talk to someone but you're busy looking over their shoulder, at the next person that's on your list of people to talk to! Some of us have the rubber-neck syndrome in life generally, How many of us want to hear the answer when we say, 'How are you?' Yet engaging with the world, identifying with the world, and expressing God's passion for people involves a change in our attitudes.

It raises the question about how we view people, whether people are acceptable or not. We pigeon-hole people so easily – this person is acceptable, this person certainly isn't. Our God is passionate about people! Hospitality is at the heart of Who God is. God welcomes us. You know, God has big arms. He welcomes us into His presence, to enjoy Him and to be with Him. That's why Jesus came, that we might have that wonderful depth, an ever-deepening relationship with God; that place of belonging, of receiving the hospitality, the welcome of our God. In a society increasingly characterised by isolation and huge pressure on the individual's sense of identity, this sort of love can reach people in ways nothing else can. It has implications for us: in taking the initiative, in welcoming people, in being people who venture out of our churches – where our churches don't have walls. It's where we take the time to hear the answers of 'How are you?', where neighbourliness is a reality.

This world needs Christians to be good news, and not just to talk about it. The word love has been distorted and diluted, when we talk about the love of God to some people. I always remember a woman in her forties who said to me, 'When you talk about the word love, what comes into my mind is my father, who abused me consistently from the age of seven to the age of fifteen. When you talk about the word love, that's all I see and hear.' That may be an extreme case, but when we use these words they mean different things to different people, and are often very far from the love that our God has – His passion for people. We are called to be people who love people with God's love.

Realism about sin

The third conviction, that we see in both the life of Christ and at the heart of the gospel, is a realism about sin. God is utterly realistic about human frailties and sinfulness but cares about us just the same. I think it's Gerald Coates that talks about the fact that God can never become disillusioned about us, because He has no illusions in the first place! We don't have to be cardboard cut-out saints. We're called to be people who love and serve our God. He understands our frailties, and is committed to working to see us changed. God is realistic about sin and the fact that it needs dealing with, in individuals and in its wider manifestations in society. That's why the centrality of the cross is so important. In Matthew chapter 5:13-16, we read that Christians are to be in the world. We're described as salt and light and that gives us some clues as to how we engage with the reality of sin around us. Salt was and is still used to prevent decay, but it's also used to bring flavour. In the colourless, flavourless world that so many of us experience, we Christians are called not just to work to arrest the decay in our society, we're also called to bring some flavour into it. Don't we have things to celebrate? Don't we have a joy that transcends and is deeper than any other joy? If our salvation means anything to us, where is celebration? We live in a world that needs celebration. You can see people hungering for it as they cheer on the football terraces. Why can't we be agents of joy in our communities and our neighbourhoods, to bring celebration?

In being realistic about sin, that means we should not become surprised or disillusioned by what goes on around us. It may cause us pain, it may cause us deep sadness, but to become disillusioned, or even to be surprised by what goes on in the world around us, and retreating into becoming negative grumblers like everybody else around us – that is not an option for us as Christians. If we are realistic about sin, we also know that there is an antidote to sin; the centrality of the cross, the good news of Jesus. The antidote to sin is grace. We are called to be bringers of grace, spilling out of us wherever we go. When someone bumps into you, what spills out? What do we leave behind us after we've been in a room, conversing with people? Do we leave something of the fragrance of the presence of Christ? Or do we leave people with a funny knotted-up feeling in the pit of their stomach, or a sour taste in their mouth, or just feeling a bit discouraged? This world needs grace-bringers, and we as Christians are recipients of the grace of the Lord Jesus Christ. He came as One Who was full of truth and grace: truth that engages with the reality of sin, grace that spills over and makes a difference; not always shouting about what's wrong, but doing something about it. Through our lives, we must demonstrate there is a better way, lending our support to those things that affirm human worth and dignity; investing in building community around us as we see fragmentation and breakdown. Community is at the heart of the Godhead. Community is what our God longs to see, as we bring grace wherever we go.

The gospel of hope

John Stott talks about the need for Christians to have two large ears. One ear to hear the heartbeat and cry of society; and the other ear to hear the voice of our God guiding us, directing us, telling us how He perceives it and how He wants us to engage with it. We talk about building bridges into the community very often in our churches; what happens when people walk across those bridges?

I won't ask how many of you have been in a bingo hall. If you go to a bingo hall, and you're not used to it, it's very alien. You don't know where you pay your money and how much you pay and what you get for your money. You don't know where to sit; you don't know how to play the game, you certainly don't understand the language. You don't know when you've won, unless somebody helps you. I have to say, and please forgive me, it's not my desire to offend anyone, that going to church for some people around, is like that! It is so alien. We live in a largely unchurched society. We need to recognise we're not in the 1950s, we are in the twenty-first century, where church is seen as irrelevant, a hobby for some, and certainly an institution not to be trusted. For a growing number of people, church is an alien experience. Therefore the challenge for us is to take the unchanging truth of the gospel and make it accessible. We need to understand the world around us and what makes people tick. The gospel of hope is a gospel that is about forgiveness and reconciliation. We need to model this in our church community life together. I love this quote here, it's anonymous

> To dwell above with saints we love
> Ah, that will then be glory
> To dwell below with saints we know
> Well that's another story!

When people come into our churches or come into contact with us as Christians, what do they experience? Are we Teflon Christians or Velcro Christians? Teflon — nothing's supposed to stick; everything slides off, are we like that in our relationships? Are we Teflon people? Or Velcro, which has that awful ripping noise as you tear it apart — are we like that in our relationships, in our committedness one to another? Are we not a holy huddle, but demonstrating the reality of God in our midst, Who transforms relationships, Who brings reconciliation, Who creates relationships across age differences, gender differences, ethnic background differences? We need to model that and live it out in the world around us.

The gospel of hope that brings reconciliation: why are we, in the church, not at the forefront of speaking out about racism in our society? Why are we not at the forefront of speaking out about ageism? You'll say to me, 'Oh, you're just being a trendy politically-correct person'. But our God is passionate about people, all people who have value and dignity and worth. Jesus died to bring all people into relationship with Himself. He died to bring about a new community of reconciliation, He died to break down the barriers. We need to be those that work for and speak out for that and live it out.

The gospel of hope is about forgiveness. Are we people that are quick to forgive? The tragedy and the heartache of holding grudges, year after year after year, that cripple and paralyse us and give a distorted view to those we meet of the reality and freedom that salvation brings. We need to be people that give new beginnings to others; forgiveness, fresh chances in our attitudes in the workplace, towards our neighbours, or those who cut us up when we're driving down the road. I talked with a woman just two days ago, called Denise, who said: 'I have never seen Christians like this. People who are enthusiastic about what they believe. People who care about the world in which I live.' That's a tragedy, that's the first time in her life she'd experienced that. There are many more Denises in the world around us.

Do we isolate ourselves because it's safer, more comfortable, less demanding, less scary? Or do we seek to be people that have an impact? Those are the choices that face us. Leighton Ford, Billy Graham's brother-in-law, said: 'Ministry is what I leave in my tracts as I concentrate on following Jesus.' The seventh Earl of Shaftesbury, the one who founded the Shaftesbury Society, with which I work, said: 'Prayer to begin, prayer to accompany, and prayer to close any undertaking for His service, is the secret of prospering in our ways.'

Please hear me: I am not talking about yet more activism! I'm not talking about Christian duty. I'm talking about lives that are so gripped with the convictions of the truth of Who our God is and what Jesus is like and the heart of the gospel, that that spills out of us, motivates us, impels us to be people that make an impact on the world around us, both in our relationships with individuals and on a wider basis. As we pray for others, as we talk with others, as we open our lives to others, as we support others, we need to be those who do it from a rootedness in a personal relationship with our God. Because the only way grace will spill out of us is as we encounter grace personally. The only way we will have passion for people which is not sentimentality or do-goodism or duty is as we encounter for ourselves first-hand God's passion for us and hear His heartbeat for the world. Our convictions will drive our priorities but only to the degree that we are personally and profoundly gripped ourselves, where the transformational nature of the gospel is impacting our lives. Because what this twenty-first century society needs is an army of ordinary Christians with faith and with convictions about an extraordinary God, that cause us to view the world differently, and so march to a different drumbeat. People of passion who are prepared to risk identifying with need around them; people from whom grace spills over, people who are utterly realistic about human frailties and care about people just the same. People who are models of extraordinary generosity of spirit and action both as individuals and collectively together. George Bernard Shaw said: 'The reasonable person adapts to the world, the unreasonable persists in trying to adapt the world around them. Therefore all progress depends on the unreasonable person.' May God make us into unreasonable people for Him, that we might impact this world!

The last word that I want to share with you is a prayer, because as we make choices about whether to isolate ourselves or to engage with and impact the world around us, we need our God. I want to pray that prayer from Ephesians chapter 3 for all of us, which points us to the bigness of the love and power of our God. Ephesians chapter 3:16:

I pray that out of his glorious riches he may strengthen (us) with power through his Spirit in (our) inner beings, so that Christ may dwell in (our) hearts through faith. I pray that (we) being rooted and established in love, may have power, together with all the saints, to grasp how wide and long and high and deep is the love of Christ, and to know this love that surpasses knowledge – that (we) may be filled to the measure of all the fulness of God. To him who is able to do immeasurably more than all we ask or imagine, according to his power that is at work within us, to him be glory in the church and in Christ Jesus throughout all generations, for ever and ever. Amen.

Marching to a Different Drumbeat: the Shape of Holiness in the Twenty-First Century

by David Smith – 2001

DAVID SMITH

Formerly pastor of Eden Baptist church in Cambridge, and Principal of Northumbria Bible College from 1990 to 1998, David Smith is currently Co-Director of the Whitefield Institute in Oxford, which supports evangelical post-graduate research in Ethics, Theology and Mission. He served in Nigeria with the Qua Iboe Mission and on his return went to the University of Aberdeen to do a Religious studies degree, followed by research into secularisation.

The Shape of Holiness in the Twenty-First Century

Introduction

Over the past couple of weeks, I've grown increasingly apprehensive about the title that I proposed, which is 'The shape of holiness in the twenty-first century'. I'm increasingly worried that that may give rise to expectations that I am unable to fulfil. I want to discuss this twenty-first century, the cultural context, within which as western Christians we are living. What are the challenges in relation to the practice of holiness in a world like this?

I want, before I begin, to acknowledge one or two sources that I've drawn upon in preparing this lecture. I've re-read a book that had a very deep influence on me as a young Christian; *Holiness, its Nature, Hindrances, Difficulties and Roots* by Bishop J.C. Ryle.[1] I also want to acknowledge the work of an American called Douglas Frank, who wrote a book in the 1980s with the title *Less than Conquerors – How Evangelicals Entered the Twentieth Century*.[2] He looks particularly at the early Keswick movement, and I've drawn on Frank's work in what I'm going to say to you this morning. I'm going to end by reflecting on Scripture, particularly the book of Revelation, and the third book is by Professor Richard Bauckham of the University of St Andrews, and is called *The Theology of the Book of Revelation*.[3] It is quite simply the best book on the book of Revelation that I've ever read, and to anyone who is a preacher, pastor or a teacher, it's a small volume that I would most warmly recommend.

My title is 'Marching to a different drumbeat; the shape of holiness in the twenty-first century'. My purpose in this lecture is to attempt to explore what it might mean in practice for Christians, in the specific context of our post-modern world, to claim that they march to a different drumbeat. More particularly, what does practical holiness

entail in a world like ours, shaped as it undoubtedly is by the powerful forces which underlie globalisation?

Before addressing these issues, I want to look back at the beginnings of the Keswick movement in order to set the questions in a
broader historical perspective. First, though, let me anticipate a
possible objection to the view implicit in my title, that holiness may
– indeed I want to argue should – take different forms at different
times, in contrasting social and cultural contexts. A critic of this might
say if Christian holiness is fundamentally a biblical concept, then surely it will be expressed and lived out in ways that are identical at all
times. The standards of the law of God and the example of Jesus never
change, and these remain our models and guides for life in the
twenty-first century just as they were for Christians living in
the Roman Empire or in medieval Europe or in a village in some
remote part of Asia relatively untouched by modernity today. Would
we not be able to recognise sisters and brothers living holy lives, wherever and whenever we met them in the world? These are important
questions and stem from a valid concern to avoid a cultural relativism
that can endanger the absolute values and standards revealed in the
gospel. The drumbeat of our title finds its source in the Christ Who is
the Lord over all cultures and calls people to follow Him from every
period of human history. When the apostle Paul – who understood
very well the need for the translation of the gospel into the forms of
different cultures – describes his ultimate aim, he says it is to proclaim
Christ so as to present everyone perfect in Him. At all times and in
every culture, Christian holiness involves following Jesus, reproducing
something of His purity and compassion and bearing witness to the
disturbing values of the kingdom that He came to unveil.

Having said this, holiness is, as the Keswick movement has always
stressed, a practical affair, related in a vital, real way to the concrete and
specific issues that arise for Christians in their particular circum-
stances. It is not something abstract and timeless but shaped in its
expression and form by the principle of the Incarnation which lies at
the heart of the gospel. To be holy, to reflect the likeness of Jesus
Christ, demands of all of us that we relate the confession that Jesus is
Lord to the actual situation in which we live and seek to bear witness.

To fail to do this, I suggest, by retaining the forms of holiness inherited from a past generation at a time of great cultural change, is to undermine practical holiness and avoid the real challenge of discipleship. The forms of Christian holiness are various, shaped by different contexts, while the essence always involves looking like Jesus. The challenge I want to address in this lecture is precisely this: what will it mean in practice to reflect Jesus – to walk like Jesus did?

Holiness as a disputed concept

The difficulties of understanding the nature of the relationship between Christianity and culture, and between the expression of Christian holiness and culture, can be illustrated by the emergence of Keswick in the 1870s. There's a good deal of evidence to suggest that those involved in founding the Convention belonged to a troubled and deeply anxious generation. Many testimonies from these years indicate that Christians were experiencing growing tensions between on the one hand their expectations of the Christian life and on the other hand the realities of failure, compromise and unhappiness which seemed to be their normal daily experience. Those who attended the first Conventions confessed that before they discovered the victorious life they were beset by problems. These are the kinds of problems – they were 'plagued by an ugly temper' or 'giving way to irritation' or again 'acting in unlovely ways toward people who are very trying'. Those who came to Keswick one hundred and twenty-five years ago openly confessed that such failures led to their Christian lives being dogged by constant worry and anxiety. There was, in other words, a mis-match between what they knew they should be as Christians and the reality of what they experienced, day by day, in their lives. This was the context in which two books originally published in America were read avidly in the United Kingdom and set in motion a series of meetings and conferences from which the Keswick movement sprang.

The two books were W.E. Boardman's book, *A Higher Life* and more importantly Mrs Hannah Whittall-Smith's *The Christian's Secret of a Happy Life*. Mrs Whittall-Smith had a particular impact: her book struck a chord with middle and upper class British evangelicals. She had herself been deeply challenged when a non-Christian had asked her why it was that Christians seemed to be such utterly miserable people. She knew that this claim was not without foundation, but she could also testify that she had had an experience which so transformed the Christian life that it enabled believers to rebut such statements. She and her husband Robert preached a gospel of victory; they had discovered the secret that Christ could lift the believer onto a higher plane, and so enable them to escape from this slough of despond.

At the time this approach to holiness was highly controversial. Bishop J.C. Ryle was the chief critic of the early Keswick movement. He deplored the love of novelty which he detected in the new movement – he lamented the tendency to despise older approaches to holiness, derived from the English puritans. 'There is', Ryle said, 'an incessant craving after any teaching that is sensational, and exciting, and rousing to the feelings. There is an unhealthy appetite for a sort of spasmodic and hysterical Christianity.' It's a controversy that has not yet died out. In a memorable phrase, Ryle protested that the new approach to spirituality introduced by people like the Whittall-Smiths was 'little better than spiritual dram drinking'. An even more serious charge was that the families of people who claimed to have received the higher life often saw no evidence of improvement in their behaviour in the home. And as a result, Ryle said, immense harm was being done to the cause of Christ.

What was the historical and social context within which these changes in the understanding of holiness were taking place? What was it about the situation in Britain in 1870s that resulted in evangelicals, then a substantial influence in British cultural life, being so anxious and unhappy? How could we explain the widespread feeling of failure which provided the fertile soil from which the preachers of the new message of the higher life were able to reap such an extraordinary harvest? Despite his criticisms of Keswick, Ryle himself was well aware of the troubled nature of the times and he freely acknowledged that the religious condition of the country seemed to him to be quite dreadful. Less than one hundred years earlier, evangelicals had been supremely confident that they stood on the edge of a period of unprecedented blessing, and that this would result in the gospel transforming the whole world; not just the religious world, but the social world and the political world. Through the nineteenth century that optimism gradually drained away. I think you can see this not only in the attitude of J.C. Ryle but in the ministry of somebody like Charles Haddon Spurgeon. Throughout his ministry, Spurgeon was supremely optimistic; he preached a very optimistic eschatology and he believed that there were great days ahead for the gospel but by the end of his life, he was overwhelmed with pessimism, sharing Ryle's sense of gloom concerning the trends he saw both in the church and wider society.

Evangelicals in Europe, in Britain in particular, and in the United States, were actually at this time facing multiple pressures. There was not one source of difficulty, there were whole series of problems, that were confronting the evangelical worldview and I want to mention three in particular.

Modern thought

First of all, there was the emergence and seemingly unstoppable progress of what people called modern thought. This was spreading throughout the western world and it seemed to undermine traditional belief in the authority of the Bible. At this time biology was a relatively new science. Palaeontology in particular raised all kinds of questions about the historicity of the biblical narratives. Evangelicals struggled to come to terms with this new worldview. It seemed that their most cherished beliefs were being dislodged from the heart of western culture. As a result of this, a gap opened up between the generations and we have many examples of people reared in devout evangelical families who began to pass through a major crisis of faith, struggling with deep doubts concerning the faith of their parents. There's a classic account in the work of Edmund Gosse, entitled *Father and Son*. Anybody who wants to understand what was happening to evangelicalism at this time would benefit from reading that book. Gosse describes how he found himself moving almost imperceptibly away from his father's beliefs, and this generational split was experienced in many evangelical homes. It's at this point that the word 'agnosticism' comes into the English language to describe a genera-tion, many reared in devoutly Christian homes, who were now alienated from the certainties of their parents and wrestling with profound religious doubts. So far as the parents were concerned – and some of us know the pain of this from personal experience – this was obviously a major cause of anxiety and it at least in part explains the unhappiness to which I've referred.

Social problems

Another cause of tension for evangelicals related to the seemingly insoluble social problems in Victorian Britain, particularly in cities like London, Sheffield and Glasgow, where thousands of people lived in conditions of squalid destitution. Among working class people there were rising demands for political and social reforms which threatened the older, hierarchical structures to which many evangelicals seemed to be wedded. Within the emergent Labour movement there were calls for the disestablishment of the Church of England, attacks on patron-age and privilege and increasingly strident demands for social justice and universal suffrage, all of which seemed to shake the foundations of the class structure of British society. The remoteness and tranquillity of Keswick – in those days a town that had been deliberately pro-moted as a resort catering for the elite of Lakeland visitors – offered relief from these pressures. Not surprisingly, very few people from the lower classes were to be found in the Convention audiences at this time. Indeed, when a few working men did appear at the beginning of the twentieth century, this drew a rather patronising comment on the fact that they were mainly factory workers, clerks and artisans.

The clash of cultures

The third source of tension was the most serious one of all. There were growing problems in simply living the Christian life in a society that seemed to be moving in a direction that undermined the fundamental ethical values of the gospel. This was the floodtide of modernity, the dawn of the modern world. Increasingly, economic values were coming to dominate society with a result that Christians found themselves living in two different worlds. One world was the private world of the family and the church and the Convention in which Christ was confessed as Lord and the Bible constituted the supreme authority. In the other, public world, the world of commerce, there people had to live – or seek to live – by a different set of values, created not by the gospel, but by consumer capitalism which reigned supreme. Christians who had grown up being shaped by the Protestant work ethic found themselves caught in a terrible tension; since to succeed in the public world they had to be willing to act on the basis of values that seemed to run directly counter to the gospel. In the public world, caution and sobriety were being replaced by impulse; thrift and simplicity were giving way to the drive to acquire things, simply because their symbolic value increased one's standing in society. Awareness of the dangers of money seemed to be dated and an obstacle to progress in a society which actively encouraged lavish spending. The result of this was that middle and upper class evangelicals experienced a dissonance between the older values and the new practices they encountered daily in the business and the professional spheres. 'As a result', says Douglas Frank, 'God's will as understood from childhood, and the value system operating in the wider society were beginning to sound like two entirely different things.'

It was in this situation that the promise of the higher life of victory over besetting sins – worry and outbursts of bad temper – was comforting. It's very revealing to discover the kind of sins that were most frequently confessed at the early Conventions. They included, 'a tattling tongue, angry looks, impatience with servants' and most remarkable of all; 'viciousness on the croquet lawn.' Women testified that the experience of the victorious life gave them new strength on those days when they felt poorly, while their husbands were able to overcome worry about the next bank failure. Robert Pearsall Smith often spoke to the aristocracy in England's great country houses and once asked, 'does the sudden pull of the bell ever give notice in the kitchen that a temper has been lost by the head of the household?' The message of the victorious life was evidently directed to those who lived upstairs and offered them a way to overcome anger with their social inferiors; to rise above the anxiety that could plague their lives if they dwelt too long on the changes that might be underway downstairs. Despite all the pressures experienced in a secularising society, one could find in Christ a peace, a joy, a power which simply lifted the soul above such cares. In Douglas Frank's words, the message of Keswick spoke to the spiritual agonies of a troubled Christian generation in its passage to modernity and it offered that generation an opportunity to transcend its agonies through the Spirit's power to indwell the Christian life with a life of perfect victory.

I am not ignoring or denying the great good that came from the early Conventions, but Bishop Ryle's theological questions about the early Keswick were valid questions. Many of the issues that he raised were – and remain – very important: for many Keswick represented a retreat in a far deeper sense than was intended by that word. David Bebbington, the historian, has said 'The adherents of Keswick were accepting that evangelicalism which had come so near to dominating the culture in mid-century was on the way to becoming an introverted sub-culture.' However, many who attended these Conventions did hear a different drumbeat and subsequently lived lives of sacrificial service for Jesus Christ, often in the far corners of the globe or in the inner cities, where they did much to restore the credibility of the gospel. If the early Keswick Conventions failed to confront the really difficult issues concerning the practice of Christianity in a secular and materialistic society, are we able to claim any greater success in the context of the new world order at the start of the twenty-first century?

Holiness in an era of globalisation

It is relatively easy, with hindsight and the help of serious historical research, to describe the social context of Victorian Britain and identify the ways in which Christians failed to engage with some of the contemporary critical issues. For us, however the crucial issue is the understanding of our time and the response we make now as Christians. I want to focus on two aspects of our contemporary culture: its de-Christianisation and secondly on globalisation.

De-Christianisation has been catalogued frequently by people like Peter Brierley and in his recent book *The Tide is Running Out*, he charts the constant drain from the churches, particularly in England. He summarises his conclusions in this way; 'We are facing, in the churches in England, a haemorrhage akin to a burst artery. Britain is full of people who used to go to church but no longer do.' Soon after that book was published, a Scottish social historian, Callum Brown, published a book with the title *The Death of Christian Britain* and concluded: 'the cycle of intergenerational renewal of Christian affiliation has been permanently disrupted, with the result that a formerly religious people have entirely forsaken organised Christianity in a sudden plunge into a truly secular condition'.

When I read those two volumes, I had to reflect on my own family. I have a sister and a brother and my wife has a sister so there are nine children in total from those marriages. They're now all in their late twenties. One out of nine is a professing Christian. That's a cause of deep heart-searching and of considerable pain, as many of you understand. But I think reading books like this encourages me in this sense that it doesn't necessarily say there's something radically wrong with this family. There are wider factors that are at work here, there's something going on in the culture, and as these authors point out, if this intergenerational transmission of faith has been broken, then clearly we face an extremely serious situation.

Alongside that, there is the growth of what we've come to know as globalisation. Since the collapse of communism in Eastern Europe and the end of the Cold War, a particular kind of market culture has spread around the globe, drawing the whole world and all its peoples increasingly within its control. Not surprisingly, this achievement, which in many ways resembles the objectives that Christians have always associated with the missionary movement, is increasingly spoken of in language that is overtly religious. Globalisation is not a matter of simply a particular type of economic activity, that's not the issue. If that was what was at stake, there wouldn't be such a major problem for us here. It is rather the promotion of a worldview, of a way of understanding people and society. It is defining human identity in terms of the consumption of goods and the identification of people with particular brands. The global market is thus much more than merely an economic factor in modern life. It extends a particular culture around the world, and promotes the view that the consumption of material goods is of the essence of human identity and purpose. Now, if anyone doubts this kind of analysis, I think they can very quickly be persuaded of its justification by simply taking note of a few themes in contemporary advertising.

Religious themes in advertising

In 1988 the American computer giant IBM produced a TV commercial which showed great throngs of humanity going about their business while a tiny caption asked the question 'Who is everywhere?' In the background the rock group REM played the anthem 'I am Superman' as IBM proceeded to identify itself with the name of God revealed to Moses as the words 'I AM' were held aloft amid the crowds.

In the same mood, an advertisement for cell phones suggested that every owner of this particular brand might now claim the divine attribute of omnipresence as it assured customers, 'You are everywhere'. I hesitate to single out one manufacturer because it's by no means unique, but Renault cars seems to have exceeded itself in this kind of advertising. A few years ago it advertised a new model with the words 'the power' over the engine and 'the glory' over the interior. It's impossible to conceive of anything closer to outright idolatry than that particular advertisement. Even as we meet here, Renault are running a promotional campaign which has a black gospel choir leaving a church, and gathering around its latest people carrier to sing its praises.

In the early 90s, a whole series of books promoting management theories employed traditional religious language, which suggested that market capitalism had not only defeated communism but had indeed become the new religion. A best-selling volume, for example, in 1992, which had a huge impact in America has a chapter with the title, 'The market's will be done'. Of even greater concern to us is the fact that among the best-selling books on management theory in America in the 1990s were titles like *God Wants You to Be Rich* and *Jesus CEO*. As one commentator observes, 'the logic of the new economy has so penetrated every aspect of post-modern western culture that material imperatives have overwhelmed and displaced every other way of imagining the world.'

We've seen that those who came to the first Keswick Convention belonged to a troubled generation and they felt deeply the tension between their Christian profession and the pressures of a materialist world. We may criticise their response to this situation, but there's a very serious question that confronts us, and it's this: are we even aware today that there is a tension between the demands of Christian discipleship and the values which drive this global economy and more and more dominate our lives?

So what exactly is Babylon?

In trying to answer this, I want to turn to the book of Revelation. I want to reflect in particular on the statement in chapter 18. I confess it's a chapter that sends a shiver down my spine every time I read it. I think if you read it in the light of our contemporary situation, it is a terrifying chapter. It describes the fall of Babylon, and there's this famous text in chapter 18:4-5. 'Come out of her, my people, so that you will not share in her sins, so that you will not receive any of her plagues, for her sins are piled up to heaven, and God has remembered her crimes.'

This is very obviously a call for separation, to leave a sphere dominated by sin and doomed under the just judgement of God. It is, to use the language of our title, an invitation to discover a different drumbeat, and join those who, despised and hated, as they will be, march in the opposite direction to the masses who trudge toward destruction. The crucial question is – what is it we are to leave? In the context of Revelation 18, the reference is to Babylon, and the whole chapter contains a chilling prophecy of her fall and complete destruction. But this doesn't help us very much. We must decipher the code to discover who or what is represented by the verbal symbol – Babylon.

I think it would be very interesting to survey the ways in which this question has been answered in the history of biblical exposition, but I'm not going to do that. I want simply to draw on personal memory and recall that in my experience, the separation demanded by this text has often been understood to refer to institutions like the church of Rome, or even the ecumenical movement. In my youth, I listened to many sermons in which it was simply taken as self-evident that the passage was to be read as a warning against recognising other professing Christians as true believers. The text was used to justify a separatist and sectarian position in the interests of doctrinal and ecclesiastical purity. Perhaps the most charitable thing one can say about such exegesis is that it was misguided. To its great credit, the Keswick movement set its face against that kind of sectarianism, and from its beginnings, promoted a broad-based unity encapsulated in the famous slogan – 'All one in Christ Jesus.'

Perhaps today in the context of the death of Christian Britain, we may be able to discover a new and a deeper unity between all Christians in which we can together listen afresh to this disturbing word of God. The starting point for a real understanding of the passage must be the question – what did it mean then? The book of Revelation, so puzzling to us, is highly contextual, and it relates very closely to the actual world in which the first readers lived. That world, like ours, was dominated by a political and economic system whose beneficiaries lauded its achievements in explicitly religious language. I'm referring, of course, to the Roman Empire which was praised as the ultimate goal of human history. Religious belief in the sanctity of Rome was reinforced in a thousand different ways, putting early Christians in a situation very similar to that which we face today.

The perspective of the book of Revelation is radically different. John's vision is shaped on the one hand by his knowledge of the glory of God as revealed in Christ. It is shaped on the other hand by an awareness of those deeply negative aspects of Rome which involved the suffering and the anguish of people who were the victims of Roman power. The glory and the prosperity of Rome was achieved at the tremendous cost of the bodies and the souls of men. In other words, it was built on slavery – chapter 18, verses 11 to 13. This is the

Babylon from which the followers of the Lamb are called out. Ancient Babylon is being used as a symbol for every system of domination which defies the authority of the holy Creator God, and arrogantly announces the end of history in the interests of those who have their hands on the levers of power. John's first readers had no difficulty in recognising the Roman Empire as a new and powerful manifestation of the evil and idolatrous spirit of Babylon. 'It was', says Bauckham, 'a Christian vision of the incomparable God exalted above all worldly power, which relativised Roman power and exposed Rome's pretensions to divinity as a dangerous delusion'.

I come back to our own central question. Just as in the first century Christians found themselves asking how it was possible to truly follow Jesus in a world in which the pagan Roman Empire filled the horizon, so we must ask, in all seriousness, whether it is possible to be Christian in the age of globalisation. We may criticise the early Keswick movement for failing to grasp the real agenda posed by the modern world, but are we any more able to be faithful in addressing the same unfinished agenda today? Are Christians in London, Moscow, New York or Beijing capable of hearing a different drumbeat, or capturing an alternative vision to the one which increasingly dominates the entire world?

The practice of holiness

If the context of the book of Revelation in the Roman Empire suggests close parallels with our globalised world today, it is worth noticing, or reminding ourselves, that the condition of the churches in this book also sounds rather familiar. We're used to the picture of the earliest churches painted in the book of Acts, and we're inclined to treat this as though it is the normative pattern for the church in the New Testament. Here we witness congregations experiencing remarkable growth in a blaze of Pentecostal glory. Thousands turn to Christ, there's a spontaneous missionary expansion in which the gospel crosses the cultural divide between the Jew and the Greek, and this triumphant progress ends with the apostle Paul in Rome, where he teaches the message of the kingdom of God without hindrance. It

looks like a success story. And with the seed of the gospel success-
fully planted at the centre of the known world, one has the
impression that it cannot be long before the task is completed and the
end of the age arrives.

But it was not to be so. By the end of the New Testament, the picture is completely changed. Revival fires have died down, they are a
past memory; the love of many has grown cold and leaders, like the
author of the book of Revelation, find themselves imprisoned for
preaching a message that is deemed to be subversive. Looking at this
scene, a contemporary sociologist might well have written a book
with the title *The Death of Christianity in Asia Minor.* The description
of the churches in Revelation chapters 2 and 3 is a gloomy one. And
it suggests that they, like us, had found the power of an economist
culture too hard to resist. We find here whole congregations idolising
material prosperity in a manner that exactly mirrored the spirit of
Rome. The letters to the seven churches make it clear that leaders
and teachers within these congregations were urging Christians to
accept a synthesis between the gospel and the culture of Rome. For
example, the group described in chapter 2 verse 15 as the Nicolaitans
were advocating a syncretism which would enable believers to keep
the Christian name, while ensuring their continued social and economic success within Roman society. Here was a policy, similar to
that we noted earlier in this lecture, of limiting Christ's Lordship to
the private sphere so that He could be praised within the church, as
long as He was excluded from the real world in which Caesar called
all the shots.

The startling truth is that such an accommodation to the Roman
worldview resulted in the living Christ withdrawing His presence
even from the church; knocking for admission from the outside, in a
final invitation to individuals who might still be able to recognise His
drumbeat. This is the context in which the call is issued. Earlier, I
quoted a commentator who said that in contemporary western culture, the imperatives of the market economy have replaced every
other way of imagining the world. This was precisely the situation in
which John's readers found themselves. The symbols of Roman power
dominated the ancient world so completely that the citizens of the

empire had internalised the ideology of Rome and simply could not imagine another kind of world. Even today, if you stand in the ruins of the Coliseum, in Rome, or go into the extraordinary building that is known as the Pantheon, or even walk along Hadrian's wall in Northumberland, you can grasp the glory of Rome and the incredible nature of its achievement. But the book of Revelation invites Christians to imagine another world, a very different kind of world. John's visions expand his readers' world and open it up to a transcendent view of reality.

Conclusion

In conclusion, what I suggest all of this means is that two thousand years later, if we follow John through the door that stands open in heaven (chapter 4:1) we discover two things. First of all, there is an exit from the insanity of the world in which we live our lives. There is a way out of the madness of our world, an alternative view of humankind and its place in the cosmos. However, a door is also clearly an entrance, and to go through this door is to go into a world where absolutely everything is different. On the other side of the door, the first thing that comes into view is the throne of God and it is in the light of that vision of God's sovereign glory that the arrogance and folly of Babylon is seen for what it really is. Here it becomes clear that both truth and the ultimate triumph belong to the once-slain Lamb of God. The visions of Revelation are thus life-giving and life-transforming; they lead us away from lies and delusion and propaganda, to truth and reality. They point toward an ultimate goal in which the holy and loving Creator promises to make everything new and finally eliminate all the causes of human misery and grief. But to catch this vision, to go through this door, is to be exposed to great danger. Because the church that marches to this drumbeat in the context of Babylon becomes a counter-cultural, subversive and even a revolutionary force.

We've considered the controversies around the concept of holiness in the 1870s and I've indicated some sympathy for the criticisms that Bishop Ryle made of the early Keswick movement.

But there is a sense in which those who advocated the higher life had actually discovered something very important. The visions of Revelation do point to another dimension of reality, above the noise and strife of a world hopelessly addicted to the idols of Mammon and Eros. However, contrary to the sermons that I had heard half a century ago, the apocalypse does not advocate sectarian withdrawal into a privatised sphere labelled 'religion'. Rather it summons us, as the worshipping people of God, to follow the Lamb in full view of the watching world; offering a public model of an alternative community which will attract those who are wearied by the lies and the deception of Babylon. Crucial to all of this is the worshipping life of the church, 'which,' says Richard Bauckham, 'is the source of resistance to the idolatries of the public world.' In its purging and renewal of the Christian imagination, and its sustaining of genuine hope through the anticipation of the time when the true God will be recognised by all the nations in the worship for which the whole of creation is destined, the book of Revelation really does sound a different drumbeat. Marching to that drumbeat involves abandoning the modern Babylon and so being ready to face the suffering that is likely to be the lot of counter-cultural subversives.

This is why we do not read very far into Revelation before we encounter the martyrs who overcame evil by the blood of the Lamb, by the word of their testimony, and because they did not love their lives so much as to shrink from death. If the parallels I have suggested here are valid, then Christians in the western world may need to take the theme of suffering for the sake of Christ far more seriously than they have needed to do for the last seventeen hundred years. Equally, if the Keswick Convention can, through its worship and teaching, allow this truly different drumbeat to be heard in the coming decades, then in God's will it may play a crucial part in the emerging mission of the western churches in the twenty-first century.

---

[1] Ryle, J.C., *Holiness – Its Nature, Hindrances, Difficulties and Roots* (London: James Clarke & Co, 1986)

[2] Frank, D.W., *Less Than Conquerors – How Evangelicals Entered the Twentieth Century* (Grand Rapids, Michigan: Eerdmans, 1986)

[3] Bauckham, R., *The Theology of the Book of Revelation* (Cambridge University Press, 1993)